To Joan and Chuck,

So that you too could "tuck the Sun and the Moon under your arms and roam the boundless Way."

A word to the wise

Stephen Lukashevich

Santa Barbara, April 1, 1997

Thus Spake Master Chuang

American University Studies

Series V
Philosophy
Vol. 25

PETER LANG
New York · Berne · Frankfurt am Main · Paris

Stephen Lukashevich

Thus Spake Master Chuang

A Structural Exegesis
of Taoist Philosophy

PETER LANG
New York · Berne · Frankfurt am Main · Paris

Library of Congress Cataloging-in-Publication Data

Lukashevich, Stephen.
Thus spake Master Chuang.

  (American University studies. Series V, Philosophy; vol. 25)
  Bibliography: p.
  Includes index.
  1. Chuang-tzu. Nan-hua ching. I. Title. II. Series:
  American university studies. Series V, Philosophy; vol. 25.
  BL1900.C576L85   1987   181'.09514   87 2871
  ISBN 0-8204-0391-3
  ISSN 0739-6392

CIP-Kurztitelaufnahme der Deutschen Bibliothek

Lukashevich, Stephen:
Thus spake master Chuang : a structural exegesis
of Taoist philosophy / Stephen Lukashevich. –
New York; Berne; Frankfurt am Main; Paris:
Lang, 1987.
  (American University Studies: Ser. 5,
  Philosophy; Vol. 25)
  ISBN 0-8204-0390-3

NE: American University Studies / 05

Grateful acknowledgement is due for permission to quote from
Burton Watson's *Chuang Tzu: Basic Writings* ©1968 Columbia University Press

Printed by Weihert-Druck GmbH, Darmstadt (West Germany)

TO OLGA

Thought-analysis invariably asks the following question: What is it that has been said in that which has been said?

Michel Foucault, *L'archéologie du savoir*

CONTENTS

ACKNOWLEDGMENTS

First of all, I want to thank the Columbia University Press for their special permission to quote from Burton Watson's translation of the *Complete Works of Chuang Tzu**. Second, I want to thank the University of Delaware for its financial assistance and, generally, for providing me with ideal working conditions. Third, I want to thank Ms. Siân Frick, who typed and corrected my manuscript. Indeed, her awesome typing virtuosity and linguistic knowledge have served me well. These acknowledgments would not be complete if I did not mention the encouragement that my friend and colleague, Professor Tai Liu, gave me throughout this work. In addition to being a specialist in English history, Professor Tai Liu is a Chinese classicist and the chief editor of a twelve-volume series on Chinese cultural history.** And, last but not least, I want to thank my muse and wife, Olga, for inspiring me and helping me with her unerring insights and suggestions. It is to her that I dedicate this book.

S.L.

Newark, Delaware

*   © 1968 Columbia University Press. By Permission.
** *New Studies in Chinese Cultural History*, 12 vols. (in Chinese, Taiwan, 1982).

INTRODUCTION

Taoism, or Philosophy of the Way (*Tao*), is one of the five important Chinese schools of thought that competed against each other before the Third Century B.C.[1] Generally speaking, of these five schools of thought only Confucianism endured, as the lasting expression of Chinese ethics. To be sure, starting with the Second Century A.D., there was a revival of interest in Taoism, as witnessed in Chinese alchemy, and in the various movements that sought, through a special diet and hygiene, as well as physical and mental exercises, to prolong life and, in some cases, to attain immortality. Again, there emerged a Taoist cult, which borrowed some Buddhist notions and became a religion. There is no doubt that latter-day Taoism was a departure from the Taoism of before the Third Century B.C.

In spite of a plethoric scholarly interest in the erstwhile Philosophy of the Way, or Taoism, very little is known about the nature of its teachings. And this for two reasons: First, the paucity and opacity of Taoist literature and, second, the failure of the scholars to unify the Taoist teachings into a coherent system of thought. Indeed, only three texts of philosophical Taoism have survived the tumult of Chinese history: (1) The *Lao Tzu*, or *Tao Te Ching* (The Virtue of the Way Classic), attributed to a certain Lao Tzu, or Lao

---

1   The *Chuang Tzu* refers to the following four schools of thought:
(a) Confucianism; the *Chuang Tzu* distinguishes between Confucius (551–479 B.C.), whom it often presents in a favorable light, and Confucianism which it mocks cruelly. The *Chuang Tzu* is particularly ruthless with the Confucianists Tseng and Shih. Strangely, the *Chuang Tzu* says nothing about Mencius (371?–288? B.C.), who was an important Confucian philosopher, before or at the time when the *Chuang Tzu* was allegedly written.
(b) Moism, or teaching of Mo-Ti (5th–4th Century B.C.?). who taught his brand of universal love and who demanded restriction of sensuality.
(c) The Hedonist School of Yang Chu (5th–4th Century B.C.?), who advocated unbridled sensuality as means to achieve health and happiness.
(d) The School of the Logicians, represented by Kung-sun Lung and Hui Shih. The latter is often the "straight man" in his debates with Chuang Tzu.

Tan, who might have been a contemporary of Confucius, but who also might have been a mythical figure. Confucius lived in the Sixth and Fifth Century B.C. (551–479 B.C.), yet linguistic analysis of the *Tao Te Ching* seems to suggest that this work might have been written as late as in the Third Century B.C. Be that as it may, the *Lao Tzu*, or *Tao Te Ching*, is a short work of about five thousand Chinese characters that is so terse and so cryptically abstruse that it has successfully defied interpretation. (2) The *Chuang Tzu* (Master Chuang), so called after its putative author and its protagonist, Chuang Chou, who, it seems, lived in the Fourth Century B.C. (3) The *Lieh Tzu* (Master Lieh), attributed to a Taoist sage mentioned in the *Chuang Tzu*, but, in all probability, a latter-day forgery (Second Century A.D.) that appeared in the wake of the revival of interest in Taoism. One should point out here that the *Lieh Tzu* is a compilation of Taoist lore, most of which is to be found in the *Chuang Tzu*, and of the hedonistic teachings of Yang Chu that the *Chuang Tzu* condemned. The lateness, the eclecticism and the shortness of the *Lieh Tzu* are so many arguments that militate against the *Lieh Tzu* as a trustworthy source of information about Taoism. Of the three Taoist texts that have been mentioned, the *Chuang Tzu* is the longest, the richest in content and, as will be demonstrated in this book, the most consistent. As such, the *Chuang Tzu* is the most appropriate text for investigating the meaning of the Philosophy of the Way, or Taoism.

Unfortunately, for over two thousand years, Chinese and other scholarship has failed to unify the Taoist teachings of the *Chuang Tzu* into a coherent system of thought and, in spite of countless commentaries and paraphrases, has failed to explain the gist and purpose of Taoism. As Arthur Waley wrote: "Attempts have been made to analyze *Chuang Tzu's* 'system'; but they result in leaving the reader with no idea of what Taoism or the book is like."[2] Worse yet, the scholars that wrote on the *Chuang Tzu* derogated their scholarship by basing their interpretation of the whole of Taoism

---

2   A. Waley, *Three Ways of Thought in Ancient China* (A Doubleday Anchor Book, Garden City, N.Y., 1956), X.

14

on the few passages that they liked best, while ignoring all passages that eluded their understanding. As H.G. Creel describes it:

> In such composite and sometimes contradictory materials, commonly cryptic at best, it has been possible to find evidence for the most divergent views. This has been going on for a good two thousand years. If two passages in the *Chuang Tzu* support a particular view, it has not always been considered necessary to mention the fact that twenty passages may repudiate it, perhaps with derision.[3]

Confronted by the staggering record of such a bimillenarian failure, modern scholarship decided to effect a strategic withdrawal by claiming that it is not possible to find any Taoist system in the *Chuang Tzu*, because the *Chuang Tzu* was written by "differing authors" at "differing times." To quote again H.G. Creel:

> A growing body of scholarship supports with careful and impressive documentation, the statement of Fung Yu-lan that both the *Chuang Tzu* and the *Lao Tzu* "are really collections of Taoist writings and sayings, made by differing persons in differing times, rather than the single work of any one person."[4]

But this is a feeble argument! Indeed, one could parody Fung Yu-Lan's statement and say that the Four Evangels and the Acts of the Apostles are "really collections of Christian writings and sayings, made by different persons in differing times." Yet, who could deny that such seemingly disconnected writings offer the basic system of Christianity?

In spite of the gloom that seems to pervade the world of the *Chuang Tzu* scholars, it is possible to demonstrate that the message of the *Chuang Tzu* represents a well-defined system of thought. Indeed, by means of the structural analysis of the text of the *Chuang Tzu*, it is possible to prove that the *Chuang Tzu* is essentially a

3   H.G. Creel, *What is Taoism? and Other Studies in Chinese Cultural History* (The University of Chicago Press, Chicago and London, 1970), p. 2.
4   *Ibid.*, pp. 1–2.

manual of pain-avoidance on the psychological, sociological and physical levels of man's experience. Although Chinese and Western scholarship has recognized the sociological and physical aspects of the message of pain-avoidance in the *Chuang Tzu*, it has failed to determine the psychological dimension of this message. Moreover, it has failed to integrate this psychology of pain-avoidance with the cosmography of the *Chuang Tzu*.

The structural analysis that forms the methodological core of this book is completely original; it does not owe its existence to any authority or to any modern literary theory, but to my combined predilection for geometry and psychology. Consequently, any marginal resemblance to any other forms of structural analysis is fortuitous or accidental.

The structural analysis of this work is a method that seeks and finds a structure, or pattern, that establishes connections between the various notions and ideas of the *Chuang Tzu*. In order to be correct, this structural pattern must be warranted by the text. Accordingly, a structural analysis that is achieved at the cost of an alien structural pattern, such as Marxism, Freudianism and other *isms* is a spurious structural analysis; it is like looking at a text through a pre-cut stencil. A genuine structural analysis must be warranted by the text, because it is only then that it can reveal the purpose and the intention of the text.[5]

At this point, I would like to explain the priming thought that gave me the notion of what the structural pattern of the *Chuang Tzu* must be. Time and again, the *Chuang Tzu* says that he who follows the Way of Heaven and Earth will avoid all harm and pain. But, as argued in the *Chuang Tzu*, the Way of Heaven and Earth is the Natural Law of the universe, that is to say, a cosmography, whereas harm- and pain-avoidance is the purview of man's consciousness and, as such, a psychology. To say, therefore, that he who follows the Way of Heaven and Earth will avoid all harm and pain means that, in addition to being the Natural Law of the universe, or cosmo-

5   For another demonstration of structural analysis, see: S. Lukashevich, *N.F. Fedorov (1828–1903): A Study in Russian Eupsychian and Utopian Thought* (University of Delaware Press, Newark, Del., 1977).

graphy, the Way of Heaven and Earth is also the macrocosm of man's consciousness and, as such, a psychology. Conversely, man's consciousness is the microcosm of the Way of Heaven and Earth and, as such, a cosmography. The *Chuang Tzu* describes the Way of Heaven and Earth as a cycle. Consequently, as the microcosm of the Way of Heaven and Earth, man's consciousness is a reduced model of the Way, that is to say, also a cycle. Finally, since man can follow the Way of Heaven and Earth and, thus, avoid all harm and pain, the cycle of man's consciousness must have access to the larger cycle of the Way. Accordingly, the structural pattern of the *Chuang Tzu* should represent the larger cycle of the Way of Heaven and Earth, as circumscribing the smaller cycle of man's consciousness.

This book will demonstrate the efficacity of this type of structural analysis in as hopeless a case as that of the *Chuang Tzu* and, in so doing, unify the teachings of the *Chuang Tzu* into a coherent system of thought. For this purpose, I have availed myself of Burton Watson's admirable translation of the complete text of the *Chuang Tzu*.[6] The numbers in square brackets, at the end of each quotation, refer to the page number of his work. Finally, since the problem of the multiple authorship of the *Chuang Tzu* may cast a pall of suspicion on the validity of my method, I have made a special point to select my quotations from all parts of the book.

6   *The Complete Works of Chuang Tzu* (Translated by Burton Watson) (Columbia University Press, New York and London, 1968).

Chapter One

THE STRUCTURE OF TAOISM

As mentioned in the Introduction, this book will demonstrate that the *Chuang Tzu's* teachings are a psychology of pain-avoidance on the psychological, sociological and physical levels of man's experience. Such an avoidance of pain is the result of man's conscious pursuit of the Way of Heaven and Earth. Nonetheless the terms "pain-avoidance" or "avoidance of pain" do not exist in the text of the *Chuang Tzu*. Yet, these terms that I use throughout my book subsume admirably what the *Chuang Tzu* means and says. Indeed, the *Chuang Tzu* says (see the block of quotations below) that he who follows the Way of Heaven and Earth avoids harm and injury. Harm and injury are notions that suggest pain on the social and physical planes of man's experience. By the same token, the *Chuang Tzu* says that he who follows the Way of Heaven and Earth experiences mental and spiritual vigor and serenity, that is to say, absence of psychological pain. Consequently, in spite of the fact that the *Chuang Tzu* does not use the expressions "pain-avoidance" or "avoidance of pain," it means them. It is therefore permissible to use them in this book:

> He who understands the Way is certain to have command of basic principles. He who has command of basic principles is certain to know how to deal with circumstances. And he who knows how to deal with circumstances will not allow things to do him harm. When a man has perfect virtue, fire cannot burn him, water cannot drown him, cold and heat cannot afflict him, birds and beasts cannot injure him. I do not say that he makes light of these things. I mean that he distinguishes between safety and danger, contents himself with fortune or misfortune, and is cautious in his comings and goings. Therefore nothing can harm him.* [182] He who

---

* *The Complete Works of Chuang Tzu*, translated by Burton Watson, (Columbia University Press, New York and London, 1968). The numbers in the square brackets refer to the pages from which the quotations have been taken.

19

follows along with [the Way] will be strong in his four limbs, keen and penetrating in intellect, sharp-eared, bright-eyed, wielding his mind without wearing it, responding to things without prejudice. [239] He who holds fast to the Way is complete in Virtue; being complete in Virtue, he is complete in body; being complete in body, he is complete in spirit; and to be complete in spirit is the Way of the sage. [135]

But the Way of Heaven and Earth is a cosmography, whereas avoidance of pain is the purview of man's consciousness. Thus, the Way of Heaven and Earth is both a cosmography and consciousness. Consequently, the structuration of the *Chuang Tzu's* philosophy of the Way, or Taoism, demands the reconciliation of the Way of Heaven and Earth as cosmography with the Way of Heaven and Earth as consciousness. In order to do so, this chapter will establish, first, the structural pattern of the Way of Heaven and Earth, as cosmography, second, the structural pattern of man's consciousness, as man's mental instrument of pain-avoidance, and, third, the combination of these two structural patterns into the basic structure of the *Chuang Tzu's* philosophy of the Way.

1. Structural Pattern of the Cosmography
of the Way of Heaven and Earth

According to the *Chuang Tzu*, the Way of Heaven and Earth is the unseen but real force that accounts for the cycle of changes and transformations in the universe:

> Does Heaven turn? Does the earth sit still? Do sun and moon compete for a place to shine? Who masterminds all this? Who pulls the strings? . . . I wonder, is there some mechanism that works it and won't let it stop? [154] Perhaps someone manipulates the cords that draw it all together, but no one has ever seen his form. Decay, growth, fullness, emptiness, now murky, now bright, the sun shifting, the moon changing phase — day after day these things proceed, yet no one has seen him bringing them about. [225] Heaven cannot help but be high, earth cannot help but be broad, the sun and moon cannot help but revolve, the ten thousand things cannot help but flourish. Is this not the Way? [239]

As such, the Way of Heaven and Earth is the Natural Law of the universe that is responsible for the creation of all things:

> When we refer to the things of creation, we speak of them as numbering ten thousand — and man is only one of them. [176] Heaven and earth are the father and mother of the ten thousand things. They join to become a body; they part to become a beginning. [198]

Since the Way of Heaven and Earth, as the Natural Law of the universe, manifests itself in Heaven (sky) through planetary cycles, and on earth through cycles of birth, life and death, the immutable principle of this unseen Way of Heaven and Earth is its cyclicality:

> The principle of following one another in orderly succession, the property of moving in alternation, turning back when they have reached the limit, beginning again when they have ended — these are inherent in things. [292] Heaven and earth are huge, but they are alike in their transformations. The ten thousand things are numerous, but they are one in their good order . . . Pervading Heaven and earth: that is the Way. [126] The Way is without beginning or end . . . [182] Beginning and end are part of a single ring and no one can comprehend its principle. [305]

And, since this unseen Way of Heaven and Earth accounts for all creation and for all the changes and transformations of the created "ten thousand things," the way of Heaven and Earth is a dynamic cycle:

> Dark and hidden, [the Way] seems not to exist and yet it is there; lush and unbounded, it possesses no form but only spirit; the ten thousand things are shepherded by it, though they do not understand it . . . [237]

According to the *Chuang Tzu*, the cycle of the Way of Heaven and Earth receives its dynamic impetus from the dialectical opposition of the force emanating from Heaven, or Perfect Yin, and of the force emanating from the Earth, or Perfect Yang, to one another. This dialectical opposition is the result of the fact that the Perfect Yin represents extreme cold and the Perfect Yang represents extreme heat:

> Perfect Yin is stern and frigid; Perfect Yang is bright and glittering. The sternness and frigidity come forth from Heaven, the brightness and glitter emerge from the earth. [225] . . . heaven and earth are forms which are large, the yin and yang are breaths which are large, and the Way is the generality that embraces them. [291]

This means that Heaven, as source of the cold Perfect Yin, and the earth, as source of the hot Perfect Yang, are dialectically opposed to one another. Accordingly, the Way of Heaven and Earth is a cycle of transformation of the forces of Heaven and Earth into one another that is animated by the dialectical opposition of the Perfect Yin and of the Perfect Yang to one another. Thus, it is possible to represent the structural pattern of the Way of Heaven and Earth as cosmography in the following diagram:

Diagram I: Structural Pattern of the Way of Heaven and Earth as Cosmography

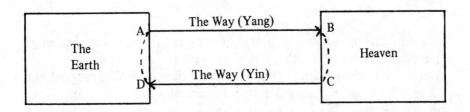

Diagram I shows that at Point B and Point D the dialectically opposed forces of the yin and yang are in unity and, consequently, in harmony with one another. Similarly, Diagram I shows that at Point C and Point A the dialectically opposed forces of the yin and yang are in separation and, consequently, in disharmony with one another. Thus, the cycle of the Way of Heaven and Earth, as the Natural Law of the universe, is a never-ending cycle of harmony and disharmony of the yin and yang. The harmony of the yin and yang results in positive occurrences, whereas the disharmony of the yin and yang results in negative occurrences:

> The yin and yang shine on each other, maim each other, heal each other; the four seasons succeed each other, give birth to each other, slaughter each other . . . The seasons have their end and beginning, the ages their changes and transformations. Bad fortune and good, tripping and tumbling, come now with what repels you, now with what you welcome. [291] [When] the yin and yang were harmonious and still, ghosts and spirits worked no mischief, the four seasons kept to their proper order, the ten thousand things knew no injury, and living creatures were free from premature death. [172] When the yin and yang go awry, then heaven and earth see astounding sights. Then we hear the crash and roll of thunder, and fire comes in the midst of rain and burns up the great pagoda tree. Delight and sorrow are there to trap man on either side so that he has no escape. Fearful and trembling, he can reach no completion. His mind is as though trussed and suspended between heaven and earth, bewildered

and lost in delusion. Profit and loss rub against each other and light the countless fires that burn up the inner harmony of the mass of men. [294–95] Man's life is a coming-together of breath [the yin and yang]. If it comes together [in harmony], there is life; if it scatters [in disharmony], there is death. [235]

According to the *Chuang Tzu*, the creation of all living things through the process of birth is the result of the harmony between the yin, which, as cold and frigid, represents the female principle, and the yang, which, as hot and fiery, represents the male principle. Thus, on the biological and physiological planes, the cosmic forces of the yin and yang reveal themselves in female and male sexuality:

> . . . the two [the female yin and the male yang] mingle, penetrate, come together, harmonize, and all things are born therefrom. [225] . . . and the ten thousand things give bodily form to one another through the process of birth. [238]

Thus, as a cycle of harmony and disharmony of the yin and yang, the Way of Heaven and Earth is a cycle of attraction and repulsion of the sexes, as well as a cycle of positive and negative phenomena:

> Desire and hatred, rejection and acceptance thereupon rise up in succession; the pairing of halves between male and female thereupon becomes a regular occurrence. Security and danger trade places with each other, bad and good fortune give birth to each other, tense times and relaxed ones buffet one another, gathering-together and scattering [of the yin and yang] bring it all to completion. [291–92]

According to the *Chuang Tzu*, the cycle of the Way of Heaven and Earth manifests itself in eight distinct cycles — the eight cycles of the Way. Incidentally, this is the first time that the notion of the eight cycles of the Way makes its appearance in the *Chuang Tzu* scholarship.

2. The Eight Cycles of the Way

a. First Cycle of the Way:

Form ⇌ Formlessness

The Way of Heaven and Earth, as the Natural Law of the universe, accounts for the existence of all things on earth. All existent things possess a form, and all existent things go through a dynamic triple cycle of: (1) Genesis/birth → (2) existence/life → (3) destruction/ death. Before their genesis/birth and after their destruction/death, things have no form. For this reason, their dynamic triple cycle of genesis/birth, existence/life and destruction/death is also the cycle of: Formlessness (before genesis/birth) → Form (after genesis/birth) → Formlessness (after destruction/death), or, simply, the cycle of: Form ⇌ Formlessness. Thus, the first cycle of the Way of Heaven and Earth that, as the Natural Law of the universe, accounts for the existence of all things on earth is: Form ⇌ Formlessness: "The formless moves to the realm of form; the formed moves back to the realm of formlessness." [240]

Lastly, since form is the result of the action of the Way of Heaven and Earth, as cycle of Form ⇌ Formlessness, the Way of Heaven and Earth possesses the attribute of formlessness:

The Way has its reality and its signs but is without . . . form. [81] That which gives form to the formed is itself formless — can you understand that? [243]

b. Second Cycle of the Way:

Limitation in Space and Time ⇌ Nonlimitation
in Space and Time

The form of a thing is its limitation in space. But the form of a thing exists only for as long as the thing that it defines and encompasses in space exists. Consequently, the form is also a limitation in time. Thus, form is a limitation in space *and* time. Conversely, formlessness is nonlimitation in space and time. Accordingly, the first cycle of the Way, namely, Form ⇌ Formlessness, accounts for the second cycle of the Way, namely, Limitation in Space and Time ⇌ Nonlimitation in Space and Time:

> Things have their limits — the so-called limits of things. The unlimited moves to the realm of limits; the limited moves to the unlimited realm. [241–42]

But, since as illustrated above, the Way of Heaven and Earth has no form, the Way of Heaven and Earth possesses the attribute of non-limitation in space and time:

> [The Way] has reality yet no place where it resides [i.e. nonlimited in space]; it has duration yet no beginning or end [i.e. nonlimited in time] . . . It has reality yet there is no place where it resides — this refers to the dimension of space. It has duration but no beginning or end — this refers to the dimension of time. [256]

c. Third Cycle of the Way:

Being ⇌ Nonbeing

Form is the perceptual proof of the existence or being of things. Conversely, the notion of formlessness implies the notion of non-existence or nonbeing. Consequently, as the cycle of transformation of form and formlessness into one another (first cycle of the Way), the Way of Heaven and Earth is also a cycle of transformation of being and nonbeing into one another:

> Who knows that being and nonbeing . . . are a single way? I will be his friend! . . . The ten thousand things [being] come forth from nonbeing. Being cannot create being out of being; inevitably it must come forth

26

from nonbeing. Nonbeing is absolute nonbeing, and it is here that the sage hides himself. [257]

Since in its third manifestation the Way is a cycle of transformation of being and nonbeing into one another, the Way, as being, came from nonbeing. Thus, at the beginning there was nonbeing; nonbeing created the Way; and the Way accounted for the being of Heaven, the Earth, and the "ten thousand things":

Before Heaven and earth existed [the Way] was there, firm from ancient times. It gave spirituality to the spirits and to God; it gave birth to Heaven and to earth. [81] In the Great Beginning, there was nonbeing; there was no being, no name. Out of it arose One [the Way]; there was One, but it had no form. Things got hold of it and came to life, and it was called Virtue. Before things had forms, they had their allotments; these were of many kinds, but not cut off from one another, and they were called fates. Out of the flow and flux, things were born, and as they grew they developed distinctive shapes; these were called forms. The forms and bodies held within them spirits, each with its own characteristics and limitations, and this was called the inborn nature. [131–32]

d. Fourth Cycle of the Way:

Life ⇌ Death

For all animated things, being signifies life and nonbeing signifies death. Accordingly, for all animated things, the third cycle of the Way, namely, Being ⇌ Nonbeing, becomes the fourth cycle of the Way, namely, Life ⇌ Death:

In the beginning there was nonbeing. Later there was life, and when there was life suddenly there was death. We look upon nonbeing as the head, on life as the body, on death as the rump. Who knows that being and non-being, life and death are a single way? I will be his friend! [257] Life is the companion of death, death is the beginning of life. [235] Life has its sproutings, death its destination, end and beginning tail one another in unbroken round, and no one has ever heard of their coming to a stop. [225]

e. Fifth Cycle of the Way:

Liveliness (fullness, motivity, turbidity, noise, and action) ⇌ Tranquility (emptiness, stillness, limpidity, silence, and inaction)

Liveliness expresses life and tranquility expresses death. Thus, the fourth cycle of the Way, namely, Life ⇌ Death, generates the fifth cycle of the Way, namely, Liveliness ⇌ Tranquility:

> Emptiness, stillness, limpidity, silence, inaction [i.e. tranquility] are the root of the ten thousand things [i.e. of life]. [143] [The Way] . . . joins with others in a hundred transformations. Already things are living or dead, round or square; no one can comprehend their source, yet here are the ten thousand things in all their stir and bustle [i.e. liveliness], just as they have been since ancient times. [236–37]

Since emptiness, stillness, limpidity, silence, and inaction collectively represent tranquility, liveliness is fullness, as well as motivity, turbidity, noise, and action. It is, therefore, possible to express the fifth cycle of the Way by the formula: Liveliness (fullness, motivity, turbidity, noise, and action) ⇌ Tranquility (emptiness, stillness, limpidity, silence, and inaction).

f. Sixth Cycle of the Way:

Multiplicity ⇌ Oneness

All created things ("the ten thousand things") possess many forms. For this reason, the notion of form is inseparable from the notion of multiplicity of forms. Conversely, the notion of formlessness is inseparable from the notion of nonmultiplicity, or oneness. Accordingly, the formula of the first cycle of the Way, namely, Form ⇌ Formlessness, produces the formula of the sixth cycle of the Way, namely, Multiplicity ⇌ Oneness: "In this world, the ten thousand things [i.e. multiplicity] come together in One. [226] The ten thousand things are really one." [236]

g. Seventh Cycle of the Way:

Diversity ⇌ Sameness

All created things ("the ten thousand things") possess many different forms. For this reason, the notion of form is inseparable from the notion of diversity of forms. Conversely, the notion of formlessness is inseparable from the notion of nondiversity, or sameness. Accordingly, the formula of the first cycle of the Way, namely, Form ⇌ Formlessness, generates the formula of the seventh cycle of the Way, namely, Diversity ⇌ Sameness:

> Differences are combined into a sameness; samenesses are broken up into differences. [290] If you look at [things] from the point of view of their differences, then there is liver and gall . . . But if you look at them from the point of view of their sameness, then the ten thousand things are all one. [69] When the ten thousand things are unified and equal, then which is short and which is long? [182]

But diversity of forms of the "ten thousand things" expresses the diversity of the qualities inherent in these "ten thousand things." In other words, diversity of the qualities of things determines their nonsameness. Consequently, the seventh cycle of the Way, namely, Diversity ⇌ Sameness, accounts for the fact that all the qualities of things tend toward their negation:

> We look on some [things] as beautiful because they are rare or unearthly; we look on others as ugly because they are foul and rotten. But the foul

and rotten may turn into the rare and unearthly, and the rare and un-earthly may turn into the foul and rotten. So it is said, You have only to comprehend the one breath that is the world. [236]

Lastly, as cycle of transformation of diversity and sameness into one another, the seventh cycle of the Way signifies that the process of creation is an indiscriminate pulping together of all life-forms and their indiscriminate re-creation in diverse life-forms:

> The ten thousand things all come from the same seed, and with their different forms they give place to one another . . . This is called Heaven the Equalizer, which is the same as the Heavenly Equality. [304—5] The seeds of things have mysterious workings. In the water they become Break Vine, on the edges of the water they become Frog's robe. If they sprout on the slopes they become Hill Slippers. If Hill Slippers get rich soil, they turn into Crow's Feet. The roots of Crow's Feet turn into maggots and their leaves turn into butterflies. Before long the butterflies are transformed and turn into insects that live under the stove; they look like snakes and their name is Ch'ü-t'o. After a thousand days, the Ch'ü-t'o insects become birds called Dried Leftover Bones. The saliva of the Dried Leftover Bones becomes Ssu-mi bugs and the Ssu-mi bugs become Vinegar Eaters. I-lo bugs are born from the Vinegar Eaters, and Huang-shuang bugs from Chiu-yu bugs. Chiu-yu bugs are born from Mou-jui bugs and Mou-jui bugs are born from Rot Grubs and Rot Grubs are born from Sheep's Groom. Sheep's Groom couples with bamboo that has not sprouted for a long while and produces Green Peace plants. Green Peace plants produce leopards and leopards produce horses and horses produce men. Men in time return again to the mysterious workings. So all creature come out of the mysterious workings and go back into them again. [195—96]

In fact, the belief in such an indiscriminate transformation of one life-form into another accounts for the following three amusing stories:

> All at once Master Yü fell ill. Master Ssu went to ask how he was. "Amazing!" said Master Yü. "The Creator is making me all crookedy like this! My back sticks up like a hunchback and my vital organs are on top of me. My chin is hidden in my navel, my shoulders are up above my head, and

30

my pigtail points at the sky. It must be some dislocation of the yin and yang!"

Yet he seemed calm at heart and unconcerned. Dragging himself haltingly to the well, he looked at his reflection and said, "My, my! So the Creator is making me all crookedy like this!"

"Do you resent it?" asked Master Ssu.

"Why no, what would I resent? If the process continues, perhaps in time he'll transform my left arm into a rooster. In that case I'll keep watch on the night. Or perhaps in time he'll transform my right arm into a crossbow pellet and I'll shoot down an owl for roasting. Or perhaps in time he'll transform my buttocks into cartwheels. Then, with my spirit for a horse, I'll climb up and go for a ride. What need will I ever have for a carriage again?" [84]

* * *

Suddenly Master Lai grew ill. Gasping and wheezing, he lay at the point of death. His wife and children gathered round in a circle and began to cry. Master Li, who had come to ask how he was, said, "Shoo! Get back! Don't disturb the process of change!"

Then he leaned against the doorway and talked to Master Lai. "How marvelous the Creator is! What is he going to make of you next? Where is he going to send you? Will he make you into a rat's liver? Will he make you into a bug's arm?"

Master Lai said, "A child, obeying his father and mother, goes wherever he is told, east or west, south or north. And the yin and yang – how much more are they to a man than father or mother! Now that they have brought me to the verge of death, if I should refuse to obey them, how perverse I would be!" [85]

* * *

Uncle Lack-Limb and Uncle Lame-Gait were seeing the sights at Dark Lord Hill and the wastes of K'un-lun, the place where the Yellow Emperor rested. Suddenly a willow sprouted out of Uncle Lame-Gait's left elbow. He looked very startled and seemed to be annoyed.

"Do you resent it?" said Uncle Lack-Limb.

"No – what is there to resent?" said Uncle Lame-Gait. "To live is to borrow. And if we borrow to live, then life must be a pile of trash. Life and death are day and night. You and I came to watch the process of change, and now change has caught up with me. Why would I have anything to resent?" [192–93]

h. Eighth Cycle of the Way:

Name ⇌ Namelessness

The diversity of forms accounts for the diversity of their names. Conversely, the notion of sameness generates the notion of namelessness. Consequently, as the cycle of transformation of the notion of diversity and sameness into one another, the seventh cycle of the Way creates the eighth cycle of the Way: Name ⇌ Namelessness:

> The ten thousand things differ in principle, but the Way shows no partiality among them [i.e. sameness], and therefore they may achieve namelessness. [290]

Thus, the eighth cycle of the Way is a cycle of transformation of name and namelessness into one another.

i. Table of the Eight Cycles of the Way of Heaven and Earth. Formulation of the Way as:

Action ⇌ Inaction

At this juncture, it is possible to assemble the eight cycles of the Way in the following table:

32

Table of the Eight Cycles of the Way of Heaven and Earth

(1)	Form	⇌	Formlessness
(2)	Limitation in Space and Time	⇌	Nonlimitation in Space and Time
(3)	Being	⇌	Nonbeing
(4)	Life	⇌	Death
(5)	Liveliness (fullness, motivity, turbidity, noise, and action)	⇌	Tranquility (emptiness, stillness, limpidity, silence, and inaction)
(6)	Multiplicity	⇌	Oneness
(7)	Diversity	⇌	Sameness
(8)	Name	⇌	Namelessness

The table above shows that the eight attributes of the left-hand column and the corresponding eight attributes in the right-hand column are dialectically opposed to one another (see below). Again, the table shows that the eight attributes of the left-hand column are the result of the corresponding eight attributes of the right-hand column and, vice versa, that the eight attributes of the right-hand column are the result of the corresponding eight attributes of the left-hand column. But the eight attributes of the left-hand column are the eight attributes of the created "ten thousand things" and, as such, the result of action. Consequently, their dialectically opposed eight attributes of the right-hand column are the result of inaction. Lastly, since the eight attributes of the left-hand column are the attributes of the created "ten thousand things" and the result of the corresponding eight attributes in the right-hand column that represent inaction, the creation of the "ten thousand things" is the result of inaction. Thus, the Way of Heaven and Earth, as the Natural Law of the universe, creates and transforms the "ten thousand things" by means of inaction:

> The inaction of Heaven is its purity, the inaction of earth is its peace. So the two inactions combine and all things are transformed and brought to birth. Wonderfully, mysteriously, there is no place they come out of. Mysteriously, wonderfully, they have no sign. Each thing minds its business

and all grow up out of inaction. So I say, Heaven and earth do nothing and there is nothing that is not done. Among men, who can get hold of this inaction? [191]

This means, of course, that in order to follow the Way of Heaven and Earth and, thus, avoid pain, man must transform his action into the creative inaction of Heaven and Earth:

What is this thing called the Way? There is the Way of Heaven, and the way of man. To rest in inaction, and command respect — this is the Way of Heaven. To engage in action and become entangled in it — this is the way of man. [125] So it is said, He who practices the Way does less every day, does less and goes on doing less, until he reaches the point where he does nothing, does nothing and yet there is nothing that is not done. [235] Thus it is that the Perfect Man does not act, the Great Sage does not move — they have perceived [the Way of] Heaven and earth . . . [236]

Thus, to act through inaction is to follow the Way of Heaven and Earth for the purpose of pain-avoidance. But more will be said about this in the course of this book.

Finally, since the active "ten thousand things" that possess the eight attributes of the left-hand column of the table above are of the earth, the Perfect Yang, or force of the earth, is an active force. Thus, in addition to being a hot and fiery force, the Perfect Yang is also an active force. Conversely, its dialectical opposite, the cold and frigid Perfect Yin, or force of Heaven, is a passive force.

At this point, it is necessary to explain that there is no contradiction between the notion of the inaction of the Way of Heaven and Earth and that of the two forces that the Yin and the Yang represent. Indeed, the Yin is the passive force of Heaven and the Yang is the active force of the Earth; and the confrontation of the Yin and Yang with one another generates the dynamic impetus of the cycle of the Way. For, as mentioned above, the Way creates through the harmonization of the Yin and Yang. Translated into our terminology, this harmonization is the result of the neutralization of the active force of the Yang by the passive force of the Yin. Such a neutralization is mechanically possible. Accordingly, the inaction of the

Way of Heaven and Earth is the product of such a harmonization/neutralization of the Yin and Yang by one another. It is therefore possible to understand the inaction of the Way of Heaven and Earth as being a dynamic equilibrium, or equipoise.

Before proceeding any further and in order to forestall obvious objections, the following must be made clear: Traditional scholarship has failed to detect the dialectical nature of *Chuang Tzu's* argument. The orthodox position on the subject of ancient Chinese thought is that the latter was based on a system of binary opposition. Such, for instance, is the position of G.E.R. Lloyd and T.K. Seung. J. Needham further tells us that the system of binary opposition entered the realm of Chinese philosophy in the 4th Century B.C.* Binary opposition refers to the static antagonism that the ancient Chinese (ancient Greeks too!) had espied between polarly opposed notions. Such a binary opposition led to the classification of phenomena under the headings of the first binary opposition of the yin and the yang, such as Heaven and Earth, cold and hot; female and male, and so on. As a quest for explaining all phenomena, the resultant philosophical endeavors were reduced to binary classification, coordination of opposites, and a system of subordination within each of the opposite groups. In contradistinction to the system of binary opposition, the *Chuang Tzu's* argument is dialectical. In order to differentiate the dialectics of the *Chuang Tzu* from the better known Hegelian and Marxian dialectics, I have designated the former as generic dialectics. Generic dialectics is a method for understanding dynamically any and all phenomena. From the point of view of generic dialectics, all phenomena are the dynamic consequence of the opposition of two forces that prevail on one another in alternation. But, if one remembers the theory of pendulum-oscillation, or that of the alternating current, then one knows that two forces that oppose one another and prevail on one another in alternation impel a cyclical motion. Accordingly, from the point of view of

---

*   G.E.R. Lloyd. *Polarity and Analogy* (Cambridge U. Press, 1966)
    T.K. Seung. *Structuralism and Hermeneutics* (Columbia U. Press, 1982)
    J. Needham. *Science and Civilization in China* (Cambridge U. Press, 1956) Vol. II.

generic dialectics, all phenomena are subjected to the dynamic cycle that results from the alternating tug-of-war between two opposed forces. In the case of the *Chuang Tzu*, all phenomena are subjected to the dynamic cycle of the Way of Heaven and Earth that results from the alternating tug-of-war between the two opposed forces of the yin and the yang. As is well known, Hegel and Marx modified generic dialectics by denying its cyclical result, and by substituting for its cyclicality an ascending or progressive line. This transformation of the cyclicality of generic dialectics into an ascending or progressive line implies the transition from the diadic dynamics of the generic dialectics resulting from the opposition of two polarly opposed forces to the Hegelian triad of thesis, antithesis and synthesis.

j. The Genesis of the Eight Cycles of the Way

As explained above, the dialectical opposition of Heaven and Earth to one another is the result of the dialectical opposition of the cold, frigid and passive Perfect Yin, or force of Heaven, to the hot, fiery and active Perfect Yang, or force of the earth. Thus, the Way of Heaven and Earth is the cycle of transformation of the dialectically opposed Heaven and Earth into one another that can be expressed by the formula: Heaven ⇌ Earth. But to say that the Way of Heaven and Earth is the cycle of transformation of the dialectically opposed Heaven and Earth into one another is not to explain the eight cycles of the Way. In order to do so, it is necessary to point out that the dialectical opposition of Heaven and Earth is the relationship that exists between the notion of whole and the notion of parts. Indeed, Heaven or sky (in Chinese, a single word designates both things) contains the earth. Consequently, Heaven represents the notion of whole and the Earth represents the notion of parts of this whole. Accordingly, it is possible to express the Way of Heaven and Earth by the amended formula: Heaven (Whole) ⇌ Earth (Parts). This new formulation of the Way explains the genesis of the eight cycles of the Way.

Since parts are parts of the whole, it can be said that the whole is the cause of its parts and, consequently, that the parts are the result of the whole. But, at the same time, the parts form the whole and, for this reason, the parts are the cause of the whole and the whole is the result of the parts. Thus, both parts and the whole are the cause and the result of one another. Accordingly, it is possible to express the relationship between the notions of parts and whole by the formula: Parts $\rightleftharpoons$ Whole. The cycle of transformation of parts and whole into one another manifests itself in eight cycles that are the eight cycles of the Way. Indeed, all parts possess their own individual form which they lose when, through synthesis, they create the whole. Thus, the creation of the whole by its parts is a transition from form to formlessness. Conversely, the creation of the parts by the whole is a transition from formlessness to the individual forms of the parts. In other words, the cycle of transformation of parts and whole into one another is also the cycle of transformation of form and formlessness into one another, or the first cycle of the Way. But, as explained above, form is limitation in space and time and formlessness is nonlimitation in space and time. Moreover, since all that exists possesses a form, being is form and nonbeing is formlessness. Similarly, since all living things possess a form, life is form and death is formlessness. Again, since all that lives possesses the attributes of liveliness (fullness, motivity, turbidity, noise, and action) and all that is dead the attributes of tranquility (emptiness, stillness, limpidity, silence, and inaction), form is liveliness and formlessness is tranquility. Furthermore, since there are many diverse forms, form possesses the attributes of multiplicity and diversity and, consequently, formlessness possesses the attributes of oneness and sameness. Finally, since forms have names, form is name and formlessness is namelessness. It is, therefore, possible to write:

Parts ⇌ Whole = Form ⇌ Formlessness (First Cycle of the Way) = Limitation in Space and Time ⇌ Nonlimitation in Space and Time (Second Cycle of the Way) = Being ⇌ Nonbeing (Third Cycle of the Way) = Life ⇌ Death (Fourth Cycle of the Way) = Liveliness (fullness, motivity, turbidity, noise, and action) ⇌ Tranquility (emptiness, stillness, limpidity, silence, and inaction) (Fifth Cycle of the Way) = Multiplicity ⇌ Oneness (Sixth Cycle of the Way) = Diversity ⇌ Sameness (Seventh Cycle of the Way) = Name ⇌ Namelessness (Eighth Cycle of the Way).

The eight cycles of the relationship between the notions of parts and whole are the eight cycles of the Way. Consequently, it is correct to say that the Way of Heaven and Earth is the cycle of transformation of Heaven, grasped as the whole, and of the Earth, grasped as parts, into one another. Hence, it is possible to represent the Way of Heaven and Earth by the formula: Heaven (Whole) ⇌ Earth (Parts).

3. The Structural Pattern of Man's Consciousness

In the Introduction, I have described how I have apprehended the *Chuang Tzu's* inherent notion of man's consciousness as being the microcosm of the Way of Heaven and Earth, and how this apprehension led me to visualize the basic structure of the *Chuang Tzu* as being the cycle of the Way of Heaven and Earth (macrocosm) circumscribing the cycle of man's consciousness (microcosm). From this, it becomes clear that, in order to have a detailed structure of the *Chuang Tzu*, it is necessary to elaborate the structure of man's consciousness. Unfortunately, while the *Chuang Tzu* says much about the relationship that exists between man's consciousness and the Way of Heaven and Earth, it does not describe the structure of man's consciousness. Accordingly, it is necessary to develop the notion of man's consciousness independently from the *Chuang Tzu*, and yet faithfully to its psychological tenets. Thus, to the extent that this independent elaboration of the structure of man's consciousness is not explicity stated in the *Chuang Tzu*, it can be viewed as a convenient prosthetic device. But, to the extent that it is vindicated by the teachings of the *Chuang Tzu*, this independently elaborated structure of man's consciousness may be viewed as the unmentioned, yet manifest product of the *Chuang Tzu* itself. Finally, I should mention here that this elaboration of the structure of man's consciousness is an original creation that owes its existence to simple logical thinking, and not to any authority. It is in my interpretation of this structure that I relied on the teachings of Otto Rank. When the time comes to acknowledge my debt to him, I will do so.

Man's consciousness is the relationship that exists between man's mental representation of himself, or the Self, and man's mental representation of his world, or Reality. Since both the Self and Reality are the two poles of man's consciousness, the relationship that exists between the Self and Reality is perforce double and inverted: it is simultaneously the consciousness of Reality from the point of view of the Self, or Reality consciousness, and the consciousness of the Self, from the point of view of Reality, or Self-consciousness. To put it differently, since man is both an inseparable part of his world and, at the same time, an autonomous entity, man's consciousness can view the Self from the point of view of Reality and Reality from the point of view of the Self. In fact, it is possible to represent the initial structure of man's consciousness in the following diagram:

Diagram II: Initial Structure of Man's Consciousness

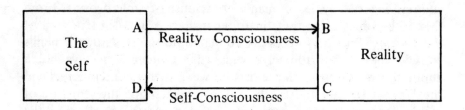

But man's consciousness is man's mental instrument for the avoidance of pain and for the pursuit of pleasure. By looking at Diagram II above, one can see that consciousness strives toward Point B and Point D and that it flees away from Point A and Point C. Accordingly, Point B and Point D are source of mental pleasure and Point A and Point C are source of mental pain. By entering these new factors into Diagram II, we obtain the second structure of man's consciousness, as illustrated in the following diagram:

Diagram III: Second Structure of Man's Consciousness

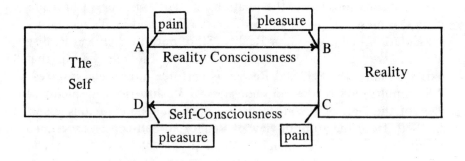

Diagram III shows the following five things:

(1) That Self-consciousness is a flight of Reality consciousness from a Reality that has become painful, and that Reality consciousness is a flight of Self-consciousness from the Self that has become painful. This means that man's consciousness is a dynamic cycle of Reality consciousness and Self-consciousness.

(2) That, as flight of Reality consciousness from a Reality that has become painful, Self-consciousness is inverted Reality consciousness. By the same token, as flight of Self-consciousness from a painful Self, Reality consciousness is inverted Self-consciousness. For this reason, Reality consciousness and Self-consciousness are in dialectical opposition to one another.

(3) That pleasure, at Point B and Point D, is the result of the unity and, therefore, of the harmony of the dialectically opposed Reality consciousness and Self-consciousness.

(4) That pain, at Point C and Point A, is the result of the separation and, therefore, of the disharmony of the dialectically opposed Reality consciousness and Self-consciousness.

(5) Lastly, that on the plane of Reality, pain at Point C is the result of pleasure at Point B, and that on the plane of the Self, pain at Point A is the result of pleasure at Point D. In Chapter Two the developed structure of man's consciousness will explain this transformation of pleasure into pain.

Finally, Diagram III above explains the *Chuang Tzu's* four techniques of pain-avoidance on the plane of man's consciousness.

The first technique of pain-avoidance is denial of either painful Reality consciousness or of painful Self-consciousness. The *Chuang Tzu* calls denial of Reality consciousness the "barring of the inside gate" and denial of Self-consciousness the "barring of the outside gate." This nomenclature is obvious. Since Reality is man's mental representation of his world, it is "outer" in relation to the Self (man's mental representation of himself); consequently, the Self is "inner" in relation to "outer" Reality. And since Reality consciousness is the consciousness of Reality from the point of view of the "inner" Self, it can be called the "inside gate" of the mind. By the same token, since Self-consciousness is the consciousness of the Self from the point of view of the "outer" Reality, it can be called the "outside gate" of the mind. Thus, for the *Chuang Tzu*, denial of painful Reality consciousness demands the "barring of the inside gate" and denial of painful Self-consciousness demands the "barring of the outside gate":

> When outside things trip you up and you can't snare and seize them, then bar the inside gate. When inside things trip you up and you can't bind and seize them, then bar the outside gate. [252]

Similarly, when both Reality consciousness and Self-consciousness are painful, pain-avoidance demands the denial of them both, or the "barring of both gates," and the surrender to one's fate (see Chapter Two):

> Have no gate, no opening, but make oneness your house and live with what cannot be avoided. Then you will be close to success. [58]

The first technique of pain-avoidance is an emergency expedient, for, in order to survive, man needs to use both Reality consciousness and Self-consciousness.

The second technique of pain-avoidance is a cyclical harmonization of Reality consciousness and Self-consciousness. Indeed, the *Chuang Tzu* condemns excessive Self-consciousness, as detrimental to Reality consciousness, and excessive Reality consciousness, as detrimental to Self-consciousness. [230–31; 218–19] Again, the *Chuang Tzu* is aware of the fact that Self-consciousness is inverted Reality consciousness and, as such, the result of the latter; consequently, the *Chuang Tzu* warns that excessive Reality consciousness could create a painfully strong opposition of Self-consciousness to Reality consciousness:

> When you're betting for tiles in an archery contest, you shoot with skill. When you're betting for fancy belt buckles, you worry about your aim. And when you're betting for real gold, you're a nervous wreck. Your skill is the same in all three cases – but because one prize means more to you than another, you let outside considerations weigh on your mind. He who looks too hard at the outside gets clumsy on the inside. [201]

Since excessive Reality consciousness and excessive Self-consciousness are detrimental to one another and yet are inversions of one another, avoidance of the pain that accrues from the opposition of Reality consciousness and Self-consciousness (Point C and Point A of Diagram III) demands their harmonization, which, as illustrated by Point B and Point D of Diagram III, is pleasurable. Thus, the second technique of pain-avoidance is a cyclical harmonization of Reality consciousness and Self-consciousness along the cycle of man's consciousness.

The third technique of pain-avoidance concerns the pain of the ambivalence of Reality and of the Self. Indeed, as Diagram III above shows, Reality is a source of pleasure, at Point B, and a source of pain, at Point C, and the Self is a source of pleasure, at Point D, and a source of pain, at Point A. Moreover, Diagram III also shows that since man's consciousness is a cycle, pleasure, at Point B, is the result of pain, at Point A, that pain, at Point C, is the result of pleasure, at Point B, that pleasure, at Point D, is the result of pain, at Point C, and, finally, that pain, at Point A, is the result of pleasure, at Point D. Thus, the pain of the ambivalence of Reality and of the Self is compounded by the pain of the confusion that arises from the permutation of pain and pleasure into one another. As the *Chuang Tzu* describes this confused state of affairs:

> Everything has its "that," everything has its "this." From the point of view of "that" you cannot see it, but through understanding you can know it. So I say, "that" comes out of "this" and "this" depends on "that" — which is to say that "this" and "that" give birth to each other. But where there is birth there must be death; where there is death there must be birth. Where there is acceptability there must be unacceptability; where there is unacceptability there must be acceptability. Where there is recognition of right there must be recognition of wrong; where there is recognition of wrong there must be recognition of right. [39–40]

Since man's consciousness is man's instrument of decision and action for pain-avoidance, it must have a unified and a clear vision of Reality and of the Self. The clarity of vision requires a neat separation of the pleasurable, or acceptable, and of the painful, or unacceptable, features of Reality and of the Self. To this effect, man's consciousness must, first, reduce itself to a single Reality consciousness and, second, to a single Self-consciousness, by means of denial of Self-consciousness ("barring the outside gate") and of Reality consciousness ("barring the inside gate"). For a single Reality consciousness would produce the vision of a single pleasurable Reality and of a single painful Self, whereas a single Self-consciousness would produce the vision of a single painful Reality and of a single pleasurable Self. As a result of such a double mental exercise, man's consciousness is in possession of two separate, distinct and static images of Reality and of the Self — one pleasurable, or acceptable, the other, painful, or unacceptable. In turn, such a situation enables man's consciousness to put an end to its ambivalence by reconciling, or better, by harmonizing the two dialectically opposed images of Reality and of the Self. But the harmonization of a pleasurable, or acceptable, Reality with a painful, or unacceptable, Reality is a harmonization of Reality consciousness and Self-consciousness, and as such it is a source of pleasure. Similarly, the harmonization of a pleasurable, or acceptable, Self with a painful, or unacceptable, Self is a harmonization of Self-consciousness with Reality consciousness, and as such it is also a source of pleasure. Thus, a clear and nonambivalent man's consciousness is both efficient and pleasurable. Lastly, since this process of clarification and unification of man's consciousness is a reconciliation, or harmonization, of Reality consciousness ("inside gate") with Self-consciousness ("outside gate"), it is possible to understand why the *Chuang Tzu* calls this third technique of pain-avoidance, the "hinge of the Way":

So the sage harmonizes with both right and wrong and rests in Heaven the Equalizer. This is called walking two roads [i.e. using single Reality consciousness and single Self-consciousness]. [41] [The sage] too recognizes a "this," but a "this" which is also "that," a "that" which is also "this." His "that" has both a right and a wrong in it; his "this" too has both a right and a wrong in it [for he has reconciled them]. So, in fact, does he still have a "this" and "that"? [i.e. an ambivalent perception?] . . . A state in which "this" and "that" no longer find their opposites is called the hinge of the Way. When the hinge is fitted into the socket, it can respond endlessly. Its right then is a single endlessness and its wrong too is a single endlessness [because consciousness is either a single Reality consciousness or a single Self-consciousness]. So, I say, the best thing to use is clarity. [40]

The fourth and last technique of pain-avoidance, on the plane of man's consciousness, is transcendence of Reality and of the Self. Indeed, Diagram III above shows that Reality is an obstacle to Reality consciousness, for it is the resistance of Reality to Reality consciousness that transforms the initial pleasure, at Point B, into pain, at Point C. Consequently, if Reality were not an obstacle to Reality consciousness, then there would not be any pain, at Point C. Similarly, Diagram III shows that the Self is an obstacle to Self-consciousness, for it is the resistance of the Self to Self-consciousness that transforms the initial pleasure, at Point D, into pain, at Point A. Consequently, if the Self were not an obstacle to Self-consciousness, then there would not be any pain, at Point A. But to say that Reality is no longer an obstacle to Reality consciousness is also to imply that Reality consciousness is able to go through and beyond Reality, or better, that Reality consciousness can transcend Reality. By the same token, to say that the Self is no longer an obstacle to Self-conscious-ness is also to imply that Self-consciousness is able to go through and beyond the Self, or better, that Self-consciousness can transcend the Self. Thus, the fourth and last technique of pain-avoidance, on the plane of man's consciousness, consists of transcending Reality and the Self. More precisely, since Self-consciousness is the flight of Reality consciousness from a Reality that has become painful at Point C, transcendence of Reality is a cancellation of both the pain at Point C and of the resultant Self-consciousness. Consequently, transcendence of Reality reduces man's consciousness to a single Reality consciousness. Again, since Reality consciousness is the flight of Self-consciousness from a Self that has become painful, at Point A, transcendence of the Self is a cancellation of both the pain, at Point A, and of the resultant Reality consciousness. Con-sequently, transcendence of the Self reduces man's consciousness to a single Self-consciousness. Thus, the *Chuang Tzu's* fourth and last technique of pain-avoidance, on the plane of man's consciousness, is another way of reducing man's dual consciousness (Reality consciousness and Self-consciousness) to a single consciousness (Reality consciousness or Self-consciousness). Since the reduction of man's consciousness to either a single Reality consciousness or a single Self-consciousness puts an end to the dynamic cycle of man's consciousness, such a "single mind" is perforce a "still" or "unchanging" mind. As the *Chuang Tzu* puts it:

> When [the mind] is unified and unchanging, this is the height of stillness. [169] Fortune and blessing gather where there is stillness. But if you do not keep still -- this is what is called sitting but [at the same time] racing [your mind] around. [58]

Similarly, since man's consciousness is the relation that exists between the Self and Reality, transcendence of either Reality or of the Self empties the mind of its dynamic content. Thus, the resultant single, still, unchanging, or inactive mind is also an empty, limpid, unroiled and, therefore, pure mind:

> When [the mind] grates against nothing [i.e. when it has transcended Reality or the Self], this is the height of emptiness. When it has no commerce with things [i.e. when it has transcended Reality], this is the height of limpidity. When it rebels against nothing [i.e. when is has transcended the Self], this is the height of purity . . . So it is said, To be pure, clean, and mixed with nothing; still, unified, and unchanging; limpid and inactive; moving with the workings of Heaven -- this is the way to care for the spirit. [169]

Finally, Diagram III shows that, since pain, at Point C and Point A, is the result of the opposition, or disharmony, of Reality consciousness and Self-consciousness, the reduction of man's consciousness to either a single Reality consciousness or Self-consciousness would remove pain, at Point C and Point A, and preserve pleasure, at Point B and Point D. According to the *Chuang Tzu*, the reduction of man's consciousness to a single, still, limpid, and pure mind accounts for both pain-avoidance and for pleasurable "inner" serenity and "outer" objectivity; in turn, with the help of a serene and objective mind, man can avoid harm:

46

Water that is still gives back a clear image of beard and eyebrows; reposing in the water level, it offers a measure to the great carpenter. And if water in stillness possesses such clarity, how much more must pure spirit. The sage's mind in stillness is the mirror of Heaven and earth, the glass of the ten thousand things. [142] The Perfect Man uses his mind like a mirror — going after nothing, welcoming nothing, responding but not storing. Therefore he can win out over things and not hurt himself. [97]

According to the *Chuang Tzu*, there is also a subconscious way to pain-avoidance. Whereas the fourth technique of pain-avoidance demands the transcendence of Reality and of the Self, the subconscious way to pain-avoidance goes one step further and demands the denial of both Reality and of the Self. Such a denial is a "fasting" of the mind, or the "emptying" of the mind, or, again, the "empty socket" that allows man's consciousness to swivel into the subconscious:

When the eye does not see, the ear does not hear, and the mind does not know, then your spirit [i.e. the subconscious mind] will protect the body, and the body will enjoy long life. [119] . . . Don't listen with your ears, listen with your mind. No, don't listen with your mind, but listen with your spirit [i.e. the subconscious mind]. Listening stops with the ears, the mind stops with recognition, but spirit is empty and waits on all things. The Way gathers in emptiness alone. Emptiness is the fasting of the mind. [57–58] Mr. Jen-hsiang held on to the empty socket and followed along to completion. [282]

As will be explained later, the subconscious mind manifests itself as conditioned reflexes on the plane of action (see Chapter Two), and as intuition on the plane of the intellect (see Chapter Three).

Finally, the *Chuang Tzu* speaks of yet another plane of man's consciousness that is far superior to either man's conscious mind or subconscious mind, namely, the "pure spirit." As will be explained shortly, "pure spirit" is the result of a permanent substitution of man's mind by the Way of Heaven, as the Natural Law of the universe.

4. Psychogenesis of the Way of Heaven (Whole) and Earth (Parts), as Means of Pain-Avoidance, and Structural Pattern of the *Chuang Tzu's* Philosophy of the Way

Diagram III above shows that mental pleasure, at Point B and Point D, is the result of the unity, or harmony, of the dialectically opposed Reality consciousness and Self-consciousness. Similarly, Diagram III shows that mental pain, at Point C and Point A, is the result of the separation, or disharmony, of the dialectically opposed Reality consciousness and Self-consciousness. Lastly, Diagram III shows that mental pain, at Point C and Point A, is the result of mental pleasure, at Point B and Point D, respectively. This means that both the pleasurable unity and the painful separation of the dialectically opposed Reality consciousness and Self-consciousness are ultimately or immediately the cause of mental pain. Accordingly, avoidance of mental pain can only be the result of a situation where there would not be either painful unity or painful separation of Reality consciousness and Self-consciousness. But absence of painful unity implies a permanent state of separation, and absence of painful separation implies a permanent state of unity of Reality consciousness and Self-consciousness. Consequently, avoidance of mental pain demands a situation where Reality and the Self would be simultaneously in unity with, and in separation from, one another. Such a situation can only be the result of the mental perception of Reality and of the Self, as separate parts of the same greater whole. Indeed, as separate parts of the same greater whole, Reality and the Self would be united by this greater whole and, at the same time, could exist as separate parts of this greater whole. Thus, avoidance of mental pain demands the mental perception of Reality and of the Self as parts of a common greater whole.

As man's mental representation of the relationship between the Self (man's mental representation of himself) and Reality (man's mental representation of his world), man's consciousness is also man's mental representation of his life-experience. Since man is an earthbound creature, man's life-experience cannot go beyond the confines of the earth. Consequently, the utmost expression of Self (man's representation of himself) and of Reality (man's mental representation of his world) is man's mental representation of the earth. Hence, the utmost expression of the notion of the greater whole of the Self and of Reality, as parts, is man's mental representation of Heaven (sky) that contains and encompasses the earth. Thus, the utmost expression of pain-avoidance is the transition from the notion of earth (parts = the Self and Reality) to Heaven (whole). But, as explained above, because parts and whole are the cause and the result of one another, the relationship between parts and whole is a cycle of transformation of parts and whole into one another that manifests itself in eight cycles — the eight cycles of the Way. Consequently, the transition from the notion of earth (parts = the Self and Reality) to Heaven (whole) for the purpose of pain-avoidance takes place along the cycle of transformation of Heaven (whole) and earth (parts) into one another, that is, along the Way of Heaven and Earth. This formulation explains the *Chuang Tzu's* assertion to the effect that he who joins the Way avoids pain.

At this juncture, it is possible to construct the basic structural pattern of the *Chuang Tzu's* ideology, that is to say, the basic structural pattern of the Philosophy of the Way, or Taoism. Indeed, to the extent that it is a mental device that man's consciousness has created for the purpose of pain-avoidance, the Way of Heaven and Earth is both a part and an extension of man's consciousness beyond its two poles of the Self and of Reality. Consequently, it is possible to imagine the Way of Heaven and Earth as a cycle that prolongs and extends man's consciousness beyond the Self and Reality. Accordingly, the relation between the Way of Heaven and Earth and man's consciousness is that of the cycle of the Way of Heaven and Earth circumscribing the cycle of man's consciousness along the vectors of Reality consciousness and of Self-consciousness. Indeed, by combining in this light the structural pattern of the Way, as given in Diagram I, with the structural pattern of man's consciousness, as given in Diagram III, we obtain the basic structural pattern of the *Chuang Tzu's* Philosophy of the Way, or Taoism:

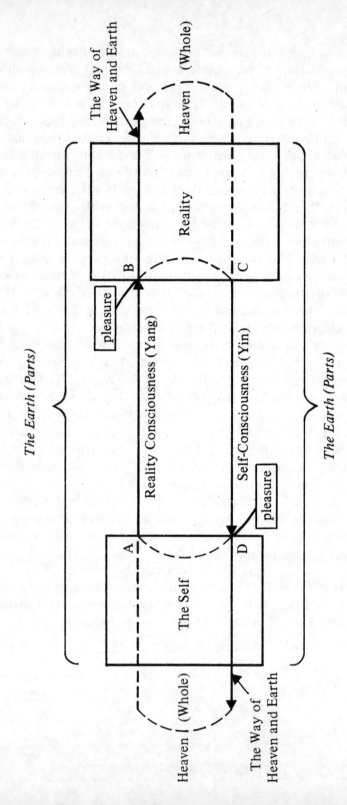

Diagram IV: Basic Structure of the *Chuang Tzu's Philosophy* of the Way, or Taoism

Diagram IV above shows that the Way of Heaven and Earth is the extension and the expansion and, therefore, the macrocosm of man's consciousness and, conversely, that man's consciousness is the microcosm of the Way of Heaven and Earth.

Diagram IV also shows that the active force of the earth, the yang, proceeds along the path of Reality consciousness and that the passive force of Heaven, the yin, proceeds along the path of Self-consciousness. This is logical. Since man acts on his world with the help of Reality consciousness, the latter is the active part of man's consciousness and, as such, akin to the "active" yang. Similarly, since Self-consciousness is a flight of consciousness from Reality (man's mental representation of his world) and, therefore, from action on his world, Self-consciousness is the passive part of man's consciousness and, as such, akin to the "passive" yin. In fact, the *Chuang Tzu* corroborates Diagram IV:

> In stillness [i.e. in "passive" Self-consciousness], he and the yin share a single Virtue; in motion [i.e. in "active" Reality consciousness], he and the yang share a single flow . . . So it is said, his movement [i.e. his "active" Reality consciousness] is of Heaven [i.e. Heavenbound], his stillness [i.e. his "passive" Self-consciousness] of earth [i.e. earthbound]. [144]

Indeed, to the extent that the Way of Heaven and Earth is the extension and the expansion and, therefore, the macrocosm of man's consciousness, Reality consciousness is the yang and Self-consciousness is the yin:

> Gentle and shy, the mind can bend the hard and strong; it can chisel and cut away, carve and polish. Its heat is that of burning fire [the yang], its coldness that of solid ice [the yin], its swiftness ["active" yang] such that, in the time it takes to lift and lower the head, it has twice swept over the four seas and beyond. At rest, it is deep-fathomed and still ["passive" yin]; in movement, it is far-flung as the heavens ["active" yang], racing and galloping out of reach of all bonds. This indeed is the mind of man! [116]

Accordingly, any and all disharmony between the yin, or Self-consciousness, and the yang, or Reality consciousness, precipitates catastrophes and calamities on man:

> There are no enemies greater than the yin and yang — because nowhere between heaven and earth can you escape from them. It is not that the yin and yang deliberately do you evil — it is your own mind that makes them act so. [256]

In particular, the *Chuang Tzu* singles out all emotions as the cause of disharmony between the yang (Reality consciousness) and the yin (Self-consciousness) and, consequently, the cause of the resultant natural upheavals:

> Are men exceedingly joyful? — they will do damage to the yang element. Are men exceedingly angry? — they will do damage to the yin. And when both yang and yin are damaged, the four seasons will not come as they should, heat and cold will fail to achieve their proper harmony, and this in turn will do harm to the bodies of men. [114]

No wonder, then, that the *Chuang Tzu* teaches complete avoidance of emotions (see Chapter Two).

Again, Diagram IV above shows that he who joins the Way of Heaven and Earth avails himself of the four techniques of pain-avoidance, on the plane of man's consciousness. More precisely, Diagram IV shows that he who joins the Way of Heaven and Earth possesses a "single" and, therefore, "still, limpid and pure mind." Indeed, the upper branch of the Way shows that man's consciousness is a single Reality consciousness and the lower branch of the Way shows that man's consciousness is a single Self-consciousness. Moreover, Diagram IV shows that the single Reality consciousness transcends Reality, and that the single Self-consciousness transcends the Self. Consequently, in addition to being "still, limpid and pure," the "single mind" of the follower of the Way is also "empty." But, as explained in the preceding section, unification of man's consciousness into either a single Reality consciousness or a single Self-consciousness, and transcendence of Reality and of the Self, are means to pain-avoidance, on the plane of man's consciousness. Furthermore, Diagram IV shows that the "single" Reality consciousness and the "single" Self-consciousness harmonize in Heaven, as a greater whole that contains the Self and Reality. Since, as explained above, such a harmonization bestows upon man's mind the mental pleasure of "inner" serenity and "outer" objectivity, the *Chuang Tzu* aptly calls the result of such a harmonization in Heaven, Heavenly joy:

> With his single mind in repose, he is king of the world; the spirits do not afflict him; his soul knows no weariness [i.e. he enjoys "inner serenity"].
> His single mind reposed, the ten thousand things submit — which is to say that his emptiness and stillness reach throughout Heaven and earth and penetrate the ten thousand things [i.e. he enjoys "outer objectivity"].
> This is what is called Heavenly joy. Heavenly joy is the mind of the sage, by which he shepherds the world. [144] . . . to harmonize [i.e. Reality consciousness and Self-consciousness] with Heaven [i.e. the notion of the greater whole] is called Heavenly joy. [143]

Finally, by representing the Way of Heaven and Earth as the macrocosm of man's consciousness, Diagram IV explains the two types of nonconscious minds that are available to the follower of the Way, namely, "spirit," or subconscious mind, and "pure spirit" which, as demonstrated in Chapter Three, is instinctual knowledge. It appears from the *Chuang Tzu* that "spirit," or subconscious mind, is the replacement of man's consciousness by the Way of Heaven, as macrocosm of man's consciousness, and "pure spirit," or instinctual mind, is the replacement of man's consciousness by the Way of Heaven, as the Natural Law of the universe. By the same token, it appears that the transition of the conscious mind to the subconscious mind, or "spirit," and the transition of the conscious mind to instinctual mind, or "pure spirit," is a question of the duration of the denial of Reality and of the Self.

Indeed, by mentally erasing Reality and the Self from Diagram IV, one would, in fact, "deny" Reality and the Self and, by the same token, the notion of Earth. In doing so, one would reduce the Way of Heaven and Earth to the Way of Heaven.

Chapter Two will demonstrate that the Way of Heaven, as subconscious mind, or "spirit," manifests itself on the plane of action as conditioned reflexes that last as long as the action lasts. Chapter Three will show that the Way of Heaven, as subconscious mind, or "spirit," manifests itself on the plane of the intellect as a sudden flash of intuition. Thus, these two chapters show that the Way of Heaven, as subconscious mind, or "spirit," is restricted to a more or less short duration.

Again, because they are part of the action, conditioned reflexes belong to the realm of perceptions. Thus, in the case of conditioned reflexes, the Way of Heaven, as macrocosm of man's consciousness, or, again, as man's subconscious mind, or "spirit," is the macrocosm of man's perceptual mind. Similarly, as a nonperceptual manifestation, intuition belongs to the realm of conceptions. Consequently, in the case of intuition, the Way of Heaven, as macrocosm of man's consciousness, or, again, as man's subconscious mind, or "spirit," is the macrocosm of man's conceptual mind (see Chapter Three). In other words, man's subconscious mind, or "spirit", can manifest itself either as subconscious perceptual mind or as subconscious conceptual mind.

In contradistinction to the subconscious mind, or "spirit," the instinctual mind, or "pure spirit," requires a protracted and arduous denial of the Self and of Reality. In order to achieve a more or less permanent denial of the Self and of Reality, man must have recourse to various forms of discipline. The *Chuang Tzu* mentions three of them. First, fasting:

> I always fast in order to still my mind. When I have fasted for three days, I no longer have any thought of congratulations or rewards, of titles or stipends. When I have fasted for five days, I no longer have any thought of praise or blame, of skill or clumsiness. And when I have fasted for seven days, I am so still that I forget I have four limbs and a form and body. [205]

Second, breathing:

> The True Man breathes with his heels; the mass of men breathe with their throats. [78] . . . Just now I appeared to him as Heaven and Earth — no name or substance to it, but still the workings, coming up from the heels. [96]

Third and last, going into a cataleptic trance, induced by self-hypnosis:

> I smash up my limbs and body, drive out perception and intellect, cast off form, do away with understanding, and make myself identical with the Great Thoroughfare. This is what I mean by sitting down and forgetting everything. [90] Confucius went to call on Lao Tan . . ., "Did my eyes play tricks on me, or was that really true? A moment ago, Sir, your form and body seemed stiff as an old dead tree, as though you had forgotten things, taken leave of men, and were standing in solitude itself!"
>
> Lao Tan said, "I was letting my mind wander in the Beginning of things" [i.e. Nonbeing]. [224–25] Body like a withered corpse, mind like dead ashes, true in the realness of knowledge, not one to go searching for reasons, dim dim, dark dark, mindless, you cannot consult with him: what kind of man is this! [237]

It seems that these three forms of discipline, namely, fasting, special breathing exercises, and self-induced, cataleptic state, are bound to produce various degrees of denial of the Self and of Reality and, by the same token, varying intensities of the instinctual mind, or "pure spirit." Unfortunately, the *Chuang Tzu* is not specific on this point. Be that as it may, these three forms of discipline prolong in time the denial of the Self and of Reality through imposition of inaction on the body and mind. In doing so, these three forms of discipline promote the replacement of man's conscious mind by the Way of Heaven, as the Natural Law of the universe, that is to say, by "pure spirit," or instinctual mind:

> You have only to rest in inaction [i.e. the comprehensive attribute of Heaven] and things will transform themselves. Smash your form and body, spit out hearing and eyesight, forget you are a thing among other things [i.e. deny Reality and the Self], and you may join in great unity with the deep and boundless [i.e. with Heaven]. Undo the mind, slough off spirit, be blank and soulless, and the ten thousand things one by one will return to the root [i.e. nonbeing as the cause of being = Third attribute of Heaven] – return to the root and not know why. Dark and undifferentiated chaos [i.e. oneness and sameness = Sixth and Seventh attributes of Heaven] – to the end of life none will depart from it. But if

you try to know it [i.e. consciously], you have already departed from it. Do not ask what its name is [for it is nameless, the Eighth attribute of Heaven], do not try to observe its form [for it is formless, the First attribute of Heaven]. Things will live naturally and of themselves [i.e. according to the Way of Heaven, as the Natural Law of the universe]. [122]

According to the *Chuang Tzu*, as the Way of Heaven, "pure spirit," or instinctual mind, protects its possessor from harm and pain:

When a drunken man falls from a carriage, though the carriage may be going very fast, he won't be killed. He has bones and joints the same as other men, and yet he is not injured as they would be, because his spirit is whole. He didn't know he was riding [i.e. he has no Reality consciousness], and he doesn't know he has fallen out [i.e. he has no Self-consciousness]. Life and death, alarm and terror do not enter his breast, and so he can bang against things without fear of injury. If he can keep himself whole like this by means of wine, how much more can he keep himself whole by means of Heaven! The sage hides himself in Heaven — hence there is nothing that can do him harm. [198–99]

Since "spirit," or subconscious mind, is the result of a more or less short denial of the Self and of Reality, and, since "pure spirit," or instinctual mind, is the result of a more or less lengthy denial of the Self and of Reality, it stands to reason that "pure spirit," or instinctual mind, is exacerbated "spirit," or subconscious mind. But, as just explained, "spirit," or subconscious mind, manifests itself either as macrocosm of the perceptual mind (conditioned reflexes) or as macrocosm of the conceptual mind (intuition). Accordingly, as exacerbated "spirit," or subconscious mind, "pure spirit," or instinctual mind, must also manifest itself either as a super-macrocosm of the perceptual mind or as a super-macrocosm of the conceptual mind. Indeed, according to the *Chuang Tzu*, the manifestation of "pure spirit," as a super-macrocosm of the perceptual mind, is the perceptual, Dionysiac ecstasy that the *Chuang Tzu* calls Dark Virtue:

If the nature is trained, you may return to Virtue, and Virtue at its highest peak is identical with the Beginning [i.e. Nonbeing]. Being identical [with

Nonbeing], you will be empty; being empty, you will be great. You may join in the cheeping and chirping [of Creation] and, when you have joined in the cheeping and chirping, you may join with Heaven and earth. Your joining is wild and confused, as though you were stupid, as though you were demented. This is called Dark Virtue. Rude and unwitting, you take part in the Great Submission. [132]

By the same token, the manifestation of "pure spirit," as a super-macrocosm of the conceptual mind, is the spiritual, Apollonian ecstasy that the *Chuang Tzu* calls Muddled Darkness:

"May I ask about the man of spirit?"
"He lets his spirit ascend and mount upon the light; with his bodily form he dissolves and is gone . . . He lives out his fate, follows to the end his true form, and rests in the joy of Heaven and earth, while the ten thousand cares melt away. So all things return to their true form [i.e. Formlessness and Nonbeing]. This is called Muddled Darkness." [137]

But ecstasies are excesses that should be avoided for the sake of the preservation of one's body and mind from harm and pain. Accordingly, the *Chuang Tzu* calls the pursuit of the Way of Heaven, as the Natural Law of the universe, that is to say, of "pure spirit," or instinctual mind, without the ecstasies of the Dionysiac, Dark Virtue or the Apollonian, Muddled Darkness, the pursuit of the Shaded or Precious Light:

Therefore understanding that rests in what it does not understand is the finest [i.e. "pure spirit," or instinctual knowledge]. Who can understand discriminations that are not spoken, the Way that is not a way? If he can understand this, he may be called the Reservoir of Heaven [i.e. as the Natural Law of the universe]. Pour into it and it is never full, dip from it and it never runs dry, and yet it does not know where the supply comes from. This is called the Shaded [or Precious] Light. [44–45]

In fact, as will be explained in Chapter Three, in the section that describes the Taoist Utopia, man's mind would become one with the Way of Heaven, as the Natural Law of the universe, when mankind returns to the state of nature.

5. Conclusion

The chief object of this chapter was to find the structure of the *Chuang Tzu's* Philosophy of the Way, or Taoism. Diagram IV above is the graphic description of this structure. Since the present work purports to explain the structural methodology that made possible the systematization of the *Chuang Tzu's* Philosophy of the Way into a coherent whole, it is pertinent to repeat the mental steps of such an undertaking.

The cornerstone of the structure of the *Chuang Tzu's* Philosophy of the Way is the *Chuang Tzu's* own declaration that the Way of Heaven and Earth is the way of pain-avoidance. Since pain-avoidance is the purview of man's consciousness and the Way of Heaven and Earth is a cosmography that embraces all Creation, the Way of Heaven and Earth, as means of pain-avoidance, must perforce be the macrocosm of man's consciousness. Conversely, this means that the structure of man's consciousness is the microcosm of the structure of the Way of Heaven and Earth.

According to the *Chuang Tzu*, the Way of Heaven and Earth is a cycle of transformation of Heaven and Earth into one another. Consequently, the structure of man's consciousness, as microcosm of the Way and as the relation between the Self (man's mental representation of himself) and of Reality (man's mental representation of his world), must necessarily be a cycle of transformation of the Self and of Reality into one another. But, as this chapter illustrates, it is possible to reach this conclusion by logical means without having recourse to the notion of the Way as macrocosm of man's consciousness.

Since the Way of Heaven and Earth is the macrocosm of man's consciousness and the way to pain-avoidance, and, since man's consciousness is the microcosm of the Way and man's mental instrument of pain-avoidance, it stands to reason that the cycle of the Way must be a part and also the extension and the expansion of the cycle of man's consciousness. This can only mean that the structure of the *Chuang Tzu's* Philosophy of the Way can be graphically represented by the cycle of the Way that circumscribes the cycle of man's consciousness. The *Chuang Tzu* warrants such a structure by stating that the yang and yin use the paths of Reality consciousness and Self-consciousness respectively, and that on the plane of man's consciousness Reality consciousness is the yang and Self-consciousness is the yin.

Again, the *Chuang Tzu's* eight cycles of the Way of Heaven and Earth and the fact that the latter is the macrocosm of man's consciousness allow us to understand the psychogenesis of the notion of the Way of Heaven and Earth as the way to pain-avoidance. Indeed, the eight cycles of the Way represent the relation that exists between the dialectically opposed notions of parts (the earth) and whole (Heaven). At the same time, the structure of man's consciousness shows that pain-avoidance requires the notion of a greater whole, of which the Self and Reality would be parts. Since man's conscious experience is of the earth (parts) and since Heaven is the greater whole that contains the earth, it becomes manifest that joining the Way of Heaven and Earth is merging one's consciousness with the greater whole of Heaven and, in so doing, ridding oneself of mental pain.

Diagram IV, which represents the structure of the *Chuang Tzu's* Philosophy of the Way, explains that by joining the Way of Heaven and Earth man's consciousness avoids mental pain, for the pursuit of the Way satisfies the four techniques of pain-avoidance, described in section 3, under Diagram III. In doing so, Diagram IV explains that he who avoids pain by means of the four techniques of pain-avoidance, on the plane of man's consciousness, also follows the Way of Heaven and Earth. Finally, Diagram IV allows us to understand the two kinds of nonconscious minds mentioned by the *Chuang Tzu*, namely, the subconscious mind, or "spirit," and the mind, as the Way of Heaven, or "pure spirit," of which more will be said in the following two chapters.

Chapter Two

PAIN-AVOIDANCE, AS PURSUIT OF THE WAY, ON THE PLANES OF THE PSYCHOLOGIES OF THE EGO, FEELING AND EMOTIONS, WILL AND ACTION

As explained in the conclusion of the preceding chapter, Diagram IV illustrates that, on the plane of man's consciousness, pursuit of pain-avoidance is also pursuit of the Way of Heaven and Earth. But, in addition to being a relation of the Self (man's mental representation of himself) with Reality (man's mental representation of his world), man's consciousness is also the Ego, feeling and emotions, will and action, by means of which the Self relates to Reality. Accordingly, this chapter continues the task of the preceding chapter by presenting and explaining the *Chuang Tzu's* prescriptions for pain-avoidance and, therefore, for the pursuit of the Way, on the planes of the psychologies of the Ego, feeling and emotions, will and action. But, in order to do so, it is necessary to develop the structure of man's consciousness, as given in Diagram III, into a structure that would represent the Ego, feeling and emotions, will and action, either explicitly or implicitly.

Diagram III in Chapter One shows that Self-consciousness is a flight of Reality consciousness from a Reality that causes mental pain, at Point C, and that Reality consciousness is a flight of Self-consciousness from a Self that causes mental pain, at Point A of the diagram. This means that Self-consciousness is inverted Reality consciousness and, vice versa, that Reality consciousness is inverted Self-consciousness. This observation is of capital importance for developing the structure of man's consciousness and, of course, for understanding the teachings of the *Chuang Tzu*.

More precisely, Reality consciousness is man's mental instrument for the pursuit of pleasure and for the avoidance of pain in man's contacts with his world. Since man's mental representation of pleasure and pain is feeling of pleasure and pain, man's Reality consciousness is first and foremost feeling. But, since it is man himself who experiences the pleasure and pain that accrue from his contacts with his world, feeling belongs to the Self (man's mental representation of himself). Again, Reality consciousness is also man's mental instrument of survival in his world. Since man survives by means of action, Reality consciousness is will to action, and, since action takes place in man's world, will to action belongs to Reality (man's mental representation of his world). Lastly, since it is man's mental instrument for the pursuit of pleasure and for the avoidance of pain in his contacts with his world, Reality consciousness must transform the requirement of feeling into an action that would result either in pleasure or in avoidance of pain. But, in order to succeed, such an action requires an adequate knowledge of the object of action and of the action itself. Consequently, Reality consciousness is also the transformation of feeling into will to action by knowledge. It is, therefore, possible to represent Reality consciousness by the following formula:

Reality Consciousness = Self → Feeling → Knowledge → Will → Reality.

And since Self-consciousness is inverted Reality consciousness, it is possible to represent Self-consciousness by the formula:

Self-Consciousness = Self ← Feeling ← Knowledge ← Will ← Reality.

By juxtaposing these two formulas of Reality consciousness and Self-consciousness, one cannot fail to notice that the Self appears to be the cause and the result of feeling. For this reason, it is tempting to conclude that the Self is feeling. But, as explained above, the Self is man's mental representation of himself, and not just perception of his actual feelings. Accordingly, it is necessary to correct this misconception of the Self, as feeling, by saying that the Self (man's representation of himself) possesses a core of feeling that we call the Ego. By entering all these new factors into the structure of Diagram III, and by reminding ourselves of the connection of man's consciousness with the pain-freeing Way of Heaven and Earth, as given in Diagram IV (see Chapter One), we obtain a new diagram that illustrates the structure of man's consciousness and that establishes its connection with the Way of Heaven and Earth.

Diagram V: Developed Structure of Man's Consciousness
and the Way of Heaven and Earth

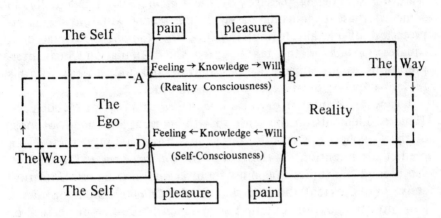

Diagram V shows that: (1) Man's consciousness is essentially Ego-psychology, because feeling, knowledge and will are the cause and the result of the Ego's relation to Reality; (2) Since the Ego is the core of feeling of the Self, Ego-psychology is a psychology of feeling on the plane of the Ego/Self; (3) By the same token, since the will is the agent of the Ego on the plane of Reality, Ego-psychology is a psychology of the will on the plane of Reality; (4) Since it is the result of Ego-feeling and Ego-will, knowledge is the subjective tool of the Ego; (5) Lastly, since it is the result of painful Ego-feeling, at Point A of the diagram, and of painful Ego-will, at Point C of the diagram, knowledge is also a flight from painful Ego-feeling and painful Ego-will. In other words, knowledge seeks to emancipate itself from painful Ego-feeling and painful Ego-will. In doing so, knowledge develops within itself an objective core, or intellect. Thus, the intellect is that part of knowledge that has freed itself from Ego-feeling and Ego-will.

The task of this chapter is to present the *Chuang Tzu's* solution to the problems of pain-avoidance on the planes of the psychologies of the Ego, feeling and emotions, will and action. Chapter Three below will deal with the problem of pain-avoidance on the plane of the intellect.

At this point, I want to acknowledge my debt to Otto Rank[1] (1884–1939) for my interpretation of Diagram V, in accordance with the supporting passages of the *Chuang Tzu*. Incidentally, in some of these supporting passages, the reader will find my interpretation of certain formulations of the *Chuang Tzu* placed in square brackets, in the text, behind the formulation. Such interpretations might appear to be wanton and unjustified; for this reason, a few words of explanation are in order.

I view my structure of the *Chuang Tzu* as a sort of Mendeleev's Table of Elements, in the sense that the correct assessment of most of the *Chuang Tzu's* cryptic statements shows that my structure can predict the intentions of the text of the *Chuang Tzu*, and, therefore, can predict the topics that must be broached in this text. Unfortunately, to the extent that the text of the *Chuang Tzu* is opaque, I have no other option but that of placing in the "empty cases" of my structure (viewed as Mendeleev's Table of Elements) those passages that seem to be best suited for my structure. Yet, in no case, have I relied on intuition, "hunches" or "lucky guesses."

---

1   Otto Rank, *Grundzüge einer genetischen Psychologie auf Grund der Psycho-analyse der Ichstruktur: I Teil* (Franz Deuticke, Leipzig und Wien, 1927).
      ———, *Will Therapy and Truth and Reality* (Alfred Knopf, New York, 1964).

1. Pain-Avoidance on the Plane of Ego Psychology:
A Rankian Interpretation

a. First Problem:

Pain of Betrayal of the Conservative Ego Caused by Changing Ego-objects

The Ego forms itself by means of feeling-identification with objects located in Reality. Indeed, the upper prong of Diagram V above shows that the Ego projects feeling onto Reality. But feeling requires an object of feeling. Consequently, Diagram V shows that the Ego projects feeling onto objects located in Reality; and, to the extent that the Ego is feeling, these objects of feeling are also Ego-objects. In turn, the projection of feeling by the Ego onto objects of feeling, or Ego-objects, is a process of objectification of Ego-feeling. The lower prong of Diagram V shows that the Ego is the result of the retrojected, objectified Ego-feeling onto the Ego. Accordingly, it is possible to say that the Ego is the product of its feeling-identification with Ego-objects located in Reality. Furthermore, the annotation at Point D of Diagram V shows that this process of Ego-formation by means of feeling-identification with Ego-objects is a pleasurable one. But the Ego-objects located in Reality (man's mental representation of his world) are mental representations of objects that are located in man's world and that are independent of the Ego. Consequently, any and all change or alteration of these objects destroys the erstwhile, pleasurable feeling of identification with them and, therefore, causes pain to the Ego. For this reason, the Ego is adverse to any change or alteration of its Ego-objects, or simply, the Ego is conservative. Thus, the first problem of Ego-pain is the problem of the pain that arises from the opposition of the conservative Ego to the change and alteration of the Ego-objects. There are three options to the solution to this first problem of Ego-pain. First, man's consciousness can deny the pain-producing, changing Ego-objects:

A man will discard the servants [i.e. his Ego-objects] who wait upon him as though they were so much earth or mud, for he knows that his own person [i.e. his Ego] is of more worth than the servants who tend it. Worth lies within yourself and no external shift will cause it to be lost.2 [262]

The denial of his pain-producing, changing Ego-objects allows man to fall back on his own Ego-ideals and, by feeling of identification with them, maintain the integrity of his Ego:

He who understands what it means to possess greatness does not seek, does not lose, does not reject, and does not change himself for the sake of things. He returns to himself and finds the inexhaustible; he follows antiquity and discovers the imperishable — this is the sincerity of the Great Man. [273]

Needless to say, the denial of the pain-producing, changing Ego-objects that are located in Reality demands the denial of Reality consciousness, or the "barring of the inside gate" (see Chapter One).

Second, man's consciousness can deny the painful Ego that results from its confrontation with changing Ego-objects by denying Self-consciousness, or by "barring the outside gate" (see Chapter One):

Meng-sun doesn't know why he lives and doesn't know why he dies. He doesn't know why he should go ahead; he doesn't know why he should fall behind [for he has no Ego/Self consciousness]. In the process of change, he has become a thing [among other things], and he is merely waiting for some other change that he doesn't yet know about. Moreover, when he is changing, how does he know that he is really changing? And when he is not changing, how does he know that he hasn't already changed? . . . in his case, though something may startle his body, it won't injure his mind; though something may alarm the house [his spirit lives in], his emotions will suffer no death. [88]

2 *The Complete Works of Chuang Tzu*, translated by Burton Watson (Columbia University Press, New York and London, 1968). Throughout the chapter, the page-number of the quotation is indicated in the square brackets that follow the quotation.

Third and last, man's consciousness can prevent the Ego-pain that results from the change or alteration of the Ego-objects by changing the Ego synchronically with the changing Ego-objects, or, in other words, by readjusting the Ego to the change of the Ego-objects. But, in order for the Ego to change apace with its changing Ego-objects, man's consciousness must have a clear Reality consciousness that demands a denial of Self-consciousness, a clear Ego- or Self-consciousness that demands denial of Reality consciousness, and the ability to adjust or harmonize Ego- or Self-consciousness with Reality consciousness that reports change of the Ego-objects. As explained in the preceding chapter, such a harmonization of a single Reality consciousness and a single Self-consciousness is the best method of pain-avoidance, and as such it is the method of the follower of the Way:

> He who changes along with things is identical with him who does not change. Where is there change? Where is there no change? [246] Joining with things, he knew no end, no beginning, no year, no season. And because he changed day by day with things, he was one with the man who never changes − so why should he ever try to stop doing this? [282] Running around accusing others [i.e. your changing Ego-objects] is not as good as laughing, and enjoying a good laugh is not as good as going along with things. Be content to go along and forget about change and then you can enter the mysterious oneness of Heaven. [88−89]

b. Second Problem:

Pain of Ego-development: The Old and the New Ego

As explained by Diagram V above, the Ego forms itself by means of feeling-identification with Ego-objects located in Reality. But, in order to do so, the Ego must first project feeling onto Ego-objects that it chooses from the many potential objects in Reality. This means that the Ego can change or alter itself at will. In fact, man's consciousness prods the Ego to do so. Indeed, Diagram V shows that feeling-identification with Ego-objects is pleasurable, at Point D, and that it becomes painful, at Point A. Accordingly, in its quest for pain-avoidance, man's consciousness urges the Ego to terminate the now painful feeling-identification and to move on to new and pleasurable feeling-identification with new Ego-objects and, consequently, on to the formation of a new Ego. Thus, in its quest for pain-avoidance, man's consciousness urges the creation of a new Ego, by means of feeling of identification with new Ego-objects, and its separation from the old Ego, by means of the abandonment of the old Ego-objects. But the abandonment of the old Ego-objects located in Reality is separation of the new Ego from them and, like all separations from Reality, it is a painful experience (see Point C of the diagram). For this reason, in its quest for pain-avoidance, man's consciousness re-establishes a new unity of feeling with the old and discarded Ego-objects, by means of such binding feeling as love, gratitude, fondness, and the like. The purpose of this unity of feeling is not Ego-formation, but avoidance of the pain that accrues from Ego-development. Lastly, since the Ego is the center of feeling of the Self, this new feeling of unity with the old and discarded Ego-objects means that the new Ego builds itself on the premises of the old Ego. As such, the Ego develops itself by preserving within itself all the stages of its development and, consequently, all the former feeling-identifications with past Ego-objects. It is in the light of what has just been said that one can understand the following statement of the *Chuang Tzu*:

> I have gone through life linked arm in arm with you, yet now you fail [to understand me] — is this not sad? You see in me, I suppose, the part that can be seen — but that part is already over and gone. For you to come looking for it, thinking it still exists, is like looking for a horse after the horsefair is over. I serve you best [i.e. through my love, gratitude, fondness, etc.] when I have utterly forgotten you [i.e. when I have discarded you as an Ego-object], and you likewise serve me best when you have utterly forgotten me. But even so, why should you repine? Even if you forget the old me, I will still possess something that will not be forgotten! [224]

2. Pain-Avoidance on the Plane of Ego-Feeling:
A Rankian Interpretation

c. Third Problem:

Pain of Contradiction between the Ego's Worldliness and
the Ego's Unworldliness

Diagram V above shows that the Ego is a cycle of feeling of worldliness and unworldliness that can be represented by the formula: Worldliness $\rightleftharpoons$ Unworldliness. Indeed, the upper prong of Diagram V shows that the Ego is the cause of the feeling of unity with Reality (man's mental representation of his world), or feeling of worldliness, and the lower prong of Diagram V shows that the Ego is the result of the feeling of separation from Reality (man's mental representation of his world), or feeling of unworldliness. Moreover, Diagram V shows that the Ego is the result of a cycle of feeling of worldliness (upper prong of the diagram) and of feeling of unworldliness (lower prong of the diagram), and that, as such, the Ego can be represented by the formula: Worldliness $\rightleftharpoons$ Unworldliness. Finally, to the extent that Reality consciousness (upper prong of the diagram) is the vehicle of the Ego's worldliness and Self-consciousness (lower prong of the diagram) is the vehicle of the Ego's unworldliness, the harmonization of worldliness and of unworldliness is a harmonization of Reality consciousness and of Self-consciousness and, as such, a source of pleasure, at Point B and Point D of the diagram: "Don't go in and hide [i.e. don't be totally unworldly]; don't come out and shine [i.e. don't be totally worldly]; stand stock-still in the middle [i.e. harmonize worldliness and unworldliness]." [202] By the same token, the disharmony of worldliness and of unworldliness is a disharmony of Reality consciousness and of Self-consciousness and, as such, a source of pain, at Point C and Point A of the diagram. In fact, the *Chuang Tzu* argues that a protracted disharmony of worldliness and of unworldliness may have fatal consequences:

In Lu there was [the unworldly] Shan Pao — he lived among the cliffs, drank only water, and didn't go after gain like other people. He went along like that for seventy years and still had the complexion of a little child. Unfortunately, he met a hungry tiger who killed him and ate him up. Then there was [the worldly] Chang Yi — there wasn't one of the great families and fancy mansions that he didn't rush off to visit. He went along like that for forty years, and then he developed an internal fever, fell ill, and died. Shan Pao looked after what was on the inside and the tiger ate up his outside. Chang Yi looked after what was on the outside and the sickness attacked him from the inside. [201–202]

d. Fourth Problem:

Pain of Contradiction between the Ego's Sociability and the Ego's Individuality

When Reality is man's mental representation of his social world, the Ego's feeling of unity with Reality, or worldliness, is a feeling of sociability and the Ego's feeling of separation from Reality, or unworldliness, is a feeling of individuality. Thus, on the plane of its relation to its social world, the Ego can be represented by the formula: Worldliness $\rightleftharpoons$ Unworldliness = Sociability $\rightleftharpoons$ Individuality. In this case, Reality consciousness that unites the Ego with Reality is the vehicle of the feeling of sociability and Self-consciousness that separates the Ego from Reality is the vehicle of the feeling of individuality. Since pleasure is the result of the harmony of Reality consciousness and Self-consciousness, the harmonization of the feeling of sociability and of individuality is also the pleasurable harmonization of Reality consciousness and of Self-consciousness and, as such, the cause of an efficient consciousness (see preceding chapter). As the *Chuang Tzu* puts it:

Who can join with others without joining with others? Who can do with others without doing with others? [i.e. who can harmonize sociability and individuality?] [86] Only the Perfect Man can wander in the world without taking sides, can follow along with men without losing himself. [300]

70

e. Fifth Problem:

Pain of Contradiction between the Ego's Participation
and the Ego's Nonparticipation in Society

On the plane of action, sociability is participation in society and individuality is nonparticipation in society. Thus, it is possible to expand the Ego's formula by writing: The Ego = Worldliness ⇌ Unworldliness = Sociability ⇌ Individuality = Participation ⇌ Nonparticipation. Since Reality consciousness is the vehicle of the feeling of social participation and Self-consciousness is the vehicle of the feeling of social nonparticipation, the harmonization of social participation and of social nonparticipation is also the pleasurable harmonization of Reality consciousness and of Self-consciousness, and the cause of efficient consciousness:

> The Perfect Man joins with others in seeking his food from the earth, his pleasures in Heaven. But he does not become embroiled with them in questions of people and things, profit and loss. He does not join them in their shady doings, he does not join them in their plots, he does not join them in their projects. Brisk and unflagging, he goes; rude and unwitting, he comes. This is what is called the basic rule of life-preservation. [253–54]

f. Sixth Problem:

Pain of Contradiction between the Ego's Conformism
and the Ego's Individualism

On the plane of behavior, sociability is conformism and individuality is nonconformism, or individualism. Thus, it is possible to extend the Ego's formula and write: The Ego = Worldliness ⇌ Unworldliness = Sociability ⇌ Individuality = Participation ⇌ Nonparticipation = Conformism ⇌ Individualism. Since Reality consciousness is the vehicle of sociability, it is also the vehicle of the feeling of conformity, or conformism, and, since Self-consciousness is the vehicle of individuality, it is also the vehicle of the feeling of individualism. Accordingly, the harmonization of conformism and of individualism is also the pleasurable harmonization of Reality consciousness and of Self-consciousness, and the cause of efficient consciousness:

> [The Great Man] will not enlist the help of others in his work, but he makes no show of being self-supporting, and he does not despise the greedy and base. His actions differ from those of the mob, but he makes no show of uniqueness or eccentricity. [178–79] Puny and small, [the sage] sticks with the rest of men. Massive and great, he perfects his Heaven alone. [75]

According to the *Chuang Tzu*, there might arise occasion when one's individualistic behavior finds social recognition; in this case, man suffers mental pain because such a recognition robs man's Ego of its individualism:

> If you move other people and make them happy, you must be showing them something unusual in yourself. And if you move others, you invariably upset your own basic nature . . . [354]

g. Seventh Problem:

Pain of Contradiction between the Ego's Altruism and the Ego's Egoism

On the ethical plane, sociability is altruism and individuality is egoism. Thus, it is possible to extend the Ego's formula to read: The Ego = Worldliness ⇌ Unworldliness = Sociability ⇌ Individuality = Participation ⇌ Nonparticipation = Conformism ⇌ Individualism = Altruism ⇌ Egoism. Since Reality consciousness is the vehicle of altruism and Self-consciousness is the vehicle of egoism, the harmonization of altruism and of egoism is also the pleasurable harmonization of Reality consciousness and of Self-consciousness, and the cause of efficient consciousness. For this reason, the *Chuang Tzu*

72

condemns exacerbated altruism, because it destroys the harmony of Reality consciousness and Self-consciousness and, as such, produces mental pain:

> He who does not look at himself but looks at others, who does not get hold of himself but gets hold of others, is getting what other men have got and failing to get what he himself has got. He finds joy in what brings joy to other men, but finds no joy in what would bring joy to himself. And if he finds joy in what brings joy to other men, but finds no joy in what would bring joy to himself, then . . . he is . . . deluded and perverse. [103]

Similarly, the *Chuang Tzu* condemns exacerbated egoism: "He who can find no room for others lacks fellow feeling, and to him who lacks fellow feeling, all men are strangers." [255]

h. Eighth Problem:

Pain of Contradiction between the Ego's Morality and the Ego's Amorality

On the moral plane, altruism is morality and egoism is amorality. Thus, it is possible to extend the Ego's formula to read: The Ego = Worldliness ⇌ Unworldliness = Sociability ⇌ Individuality = Participation ⇌ Nonparticipation = Conformism ⇌ Individualism = Altruism ⇌ Egoism = Morality ⇌ Amorality. According to the *Chuang Tzu*, morality is the extension of love and fairness to all members of the society; for this reason, the *Chuang Tzu* calls morality, benevolence and righteousness:

> What seems to apply only to intimate relationship and yet must be broadened − benevolence. What seems to apply only to distant relationships and yet must be observed − righteousness. [124] . . . to embrace universal love and be without partisanship − this is the true form of benevolence and righteousness. [149]

Conversely, amorality is nonbenevolence and nonrighteousness. Because Reality consciousness is the vehicle of the feeling of worldliness, sociability, social participation, and altruism, it is also the vehicle of the moral feeling of benevolence and of righteousness. By the same token, since Self-consciousness is the vehicle of the feeling of unworldliness, individuality, social nonparticipation, and egoism, it is also the vehicle of the amoral feeling of nonbenevolence and of nonrighteousness. Consequently, the harmonization of morality (benevolence and righteousness) with amorality (nonbenevolence and nonrighteousness) is also the pleasurable harmonization of Reality consciousness and of Self-consciousness, and the cause of efficient consciousness:

> If I am not benevolent, I harm others; but if I am benevolent, then on the contrary I make trouble for myself. If I am not righteous, I do injury to others; but if I am righteous, then on the contrary I distress myself. [252] Therefore the Great Man in his actions will not harm others, but he makes no show of benevolence or charity. [178] [The sage] accords with benevolence but does not set great store by it. He draws close to righteousness but does not labor over it. [125] So [the True Man] makes sure that there is nothing he is very close to, and nothing he is very distant with. Embracing virtue, infused with harmony, he follows along with the world . . . [276–77]

i. Ninth Problem:

Pain of Contradiction between the Ego's Sensuality and the Ego's Spirituality

When Reality is man's mental representation of his biological and physiological world, the feeling that unites the Ego with Reality (see upper prong of Diagram V) is sensuality, for the satisfaction of biological and physiological needs is the purview of the senses. By the same token, the feeling that separates the Ego from Reality (see lower prong of Diagram V) is a flight from sensuality and is, therefore, feeling of spirituality. Since Reality consciousness is the vehicle of the Ego's sensuality and Self-consciousness is the vehicle of the Ego's spirituality, the harmonization of the Ego's sensuality with the Ego's spirituality also accounts for the pleasurable harmonization of Reality consciousness and of Self-consciousness and, consequently, for an efficient consciousness. Conversely, any and all disharmony between the Ego's sensuality and the Ego's spirituality is also a painful disharmony of Reality consciousness and of Self-consciousness:

> If you try to fulfill all your appetites and desires and indulge your likes and dislikes, then you bring affliction to the true form of your inborn nature and fate. And if you try to deny your appetites and desires and forcibly change your likes and dislikes, then you bring affliction to your ears and eyes. [261]

According to the *Chuang Tzu*, harmony of sensuality and of spirituality means two things. First, it means no frustration of one's sensuality by spirituality:

> "I know that's what I should do," said Prince Mou. "But I can't overcome my inclinations."
> "If you can't overcome your inclinations, then follow them!" said Chan Tzu.
> "But won't that do harm to the spirit?"
> "If you can't overcome your inclinations and yet you try to force yourself not to follow them, this is to do a double injury to yourself. Men who do such double injury to themselves are never found in the ranks of the long-lived!" [318] No man who is incapable of gratifying his desires and cherishing the years fate has given him can be called a master of the Way. [330–31]

And second, it means no licentiousness that would injure man's spirituality:

> Now you, as sole ruler of this land of ten thousand chariots, may tax the resources of the entire populace of your realm in nourishing the appetites of your ears and eyes, your nose and mouth. But the spirit will not permit such a way of life. The spirit loves harmony and hates licentiousness.

Licentiousness is a kind of sickness . . . I just wonder, my lord, how aware you are of your own sickness. [263]

To repeat what has been said in this section that deals with the problem of pain-avoidance on the plane of the psychology of feeling: Since Reality consciousness is the vehicle of the Ego's feeling of unity with Reality, and Self-consciousness is the vehicle of the Ego's feeling of separation from Reality, the dialectical opposition of Reality consciousness and of Self-consciousness creates a dialectical opposition of feeling within the Ego. More precisely, when Reality is man's mental representation of his world, this dialectical opposition of feeling within the Ego is that of feeling of worldliness and of feeling of unworldliness. When Reality is man's mental representation of his social milieu, this dialectical opposition of feeling within the Ego is that of feeling of sociability and of the feeling of individuality. In turn, the dialectical opposition of the feeling of sociability and of the feeling of individuality becomes the dialectical opposition of the feeling of social participation and of the feeling of social nonparticipation on the plane of action; it becomes the dialectical opposition of the feeling of conformism and of the feeling of individualism on the plane of behavior; it becomes the dialectical opposition of the feeling of altruism and of the feeling of egoism on the ethical plane; and, lastly, on the moral plane, it becomes the dialectical opposition of the feeling of morality and of the feeling of amorality. Finally, when Reality is man's mental representation of his biological and physiological world, this dialectical opposition of feeling within the Ego is that of the feeling of sensuality and of the feeling of spirituality. Since the dialectically opposed Reality consciousness and Self-consciousness are the vehicles of the dialectically opposed feelings within the Ego, the reconciliation, or harmonization, of the dialectically opposed feelings within the Ego is also the reconciliation, or harmonization, of the dialectically opposed Reality consciousness and Self-consciousness. But, as explained in the preceding chapter, the reconciliation, or harmonization, of the dialectically opposed Reality consciousness and Self-consciousness puts an end to the mental pain that results from their opposition and, thus, causes pleasure. Indeed, Diagram III in the preceding chapter, as well as Diagram V in this chapter, show that the unity, or harmony, of the dialectically opposed Reality consciousness and Self-consciousness is a source of pleasure, at Point B and Point D. And, by the same token, that the disunity, or disharmony, of the dialectically opposed Reality consciousness and Self-consciousness is a source of pain, at Point C and Point A. Thus, the reconciliation, or harmonization, of the dialectically opposed feelings within the Ego is also the reconciliation, or harmonization, of the dialectically opposed Reality consciousness and Self-consciousness, and as such it is pain-avoidance and a source of pleasure. As illustrated above, the *Chuang Tzu* recommends such a reconciliation, or harmonization, of the dialectically opposed feelings within the Ego.

3. Pain-Avoidance on the Plane of the Psychology of Emotions: A Rankian Interpretation

j. Tenth Problem:

Pain of Emotions

Diagram V above bears no mention of emotions, yet it goes a long way toward explaining them. Diagram V shows that the Ego (center of feeling of the Self) acts on Reality by means of the will, at Point B of the diagram, and that the repulsion of the will by Reality, at Point C of the diagram, generates feeling. But the repulsion of the will by Reality also generates emotions. Indeed, since it is the mental mechanism that triggers off and carries on action, will to action is mental energy. Consequently, the repression of the will by Reality, at Point C of the diagram, also represents a repression of mental energy. In other words, the repulsion of the will by Reality is simultaneously generation of feeling and repression of the mental energy of the will toward the Ego. It is the combination of feeling and of the more or less violent inner tension that results from the repression of the mental energy of the will by Reality that produces emotions. Indeed, any and all emotional states are first and foremost states of inner tension that are qualified by the accompanying feeling. According to Diagram V above, emotions, as combination of repressed mental energy of the will and feeling, are, at first, a source of pleasure, at Point D, and a source of pain, at Point A. From the point of view of emotions, as repressed mental energy of the will, this means that emotional pleasure and emotional pain represent varying degrees of inner tension that the repression of the mental energy of the will by Reality generates in man's Ego. In other words, a certain amount of this tension renders the emotions pleasurable, while too much tension renders them painful, regardless of the accompanying feeling. For this reason, emotions create confusion in man's mind, as witnessed by the phenomena of tears of joy or laughter in grief. In turn, mental confusion is a source of mental pain. According to the *Chuang Tzu*, the obvious solution to the problem of mental pain, caused by emotions, is to have no emotions at all:

> The agitation of grief and sorrow, the solace of contentment and joy — these bring no enlightenment to the body. The shock of fear and terror, the elation of happiness and delight — these bring no enlightenment to the mind. [335–36] So it is said, Grief and happiness are perversions of Virtue; joy and anger are transgressions of the Way; love and hate are offenses against Virtue. When the mind is without care or joy, this is the height of Virtue. [169] . . . to serve your own mind so that sadness or joy do not sway or move it . . . — this is the perfection of virtue. [60]

Since emotions are a combination of repressed will and of feeling, avoidance of emotions is avoidance of the repression of the will and avoidance of feeling that generates the will. The next section deals with the problem of pain-avoidance on the plane of the will to action and Reality, and shows how, according to the *Chuang Tzu*, man can will and act without incurring the danger of the repulsion or "blunting" of his will to action by Reality. Accordingly, this section will only deal with the problem of the avoidance of feeling that generates the will, which, in turn, produces emotions in contact with Reality. Indeed, since will to action is essentially will to change Reality (man's mental representation of his world), avoidance of the feeling that generates will to action and the ensuing emotions is denial of the feeling that Reality must be changed. Such a denial of the feeling that Reality must be changed is also a denial of one's feeling of satisfaction or dissatisfaction with things. In positive terms, such a denial of the feeling that Reality must be changed is an unconditional acceptance of Reality, as it is (cf. Hegel's *"Was ist, ist gut"*):

> Hui Tzu said to Chuang Tzu, "Can a man really be without feelings?"
> Chuang Tzu: "Yes."
> Hui Tzu: "But a man who has no feelings — how can you call him a man?"
> Chuang Tzu: "The Way gave him a face; Heaven gave him a form — why can't you call him a man?"
> Hui Tzu: "But if you've already called him a man, how can he be without feelings?"

Chuang Tzu: "That's not what I mean by feelings. When I talk about having no feelings, I mean that a man doesn't allow likes or dislikes to get in and do him [emotional] harm. He just lets things be the way they are and doesn't try to help life along [by changing Reality]."

Hui Tzu: "If he doesn't try to help life along [by changing Reality], then how can he keep himself alive?"

Chuang Tzu: "The Way gave him a face; Heaven gave him a form. He doesn't let likes or dislikes get in and do him [emotional] harm . . ." [75–76]

However, when acceptance of Reality is not possible, the *Chuang Tzu* urges his readers to ignore situations that might demand emotional involvement:

Ah, how I pitied those men who destroy themselves! Then again, I pitied those who pity others; and again, I pitied those who pity those who pity others. But all that was long ago. [271]

* * * * *

Shih Ch'eng-ch'i went to see Lao Tzu. "I had heard that you were a sage," he said, . . ."Now that I see you, though, I find you are no sage at all. Rat holes heaped with leftover grain and yet you turn your little sister out of the house, an unkind act indeed! . . ." Lao Tzu looked blank and made no reply. [150]

* * * * *

When the springs dry up and the fish are left stranded on the ground, they spew each other with moisture and wet each other down with spit – but it would be much better if they could forget each other in the rivers and lakes! [163]

Again, since the Ego is the core or center of feeling of the Self, denial of the feeling that generates will to action and the ensuing emotions is denial of the Ego. In turn, since the Ego is the core or center of feeling of the Self, denial of the Ego is denial of the Self, and as such it is the "emptying" of man's consciousness. But, as explained in the preceding chapter, such an "empty" mind is an objective mind that allows man to avoid pain:

If a man, having lashed two hulls together, is crossing a river, and an empty boat happens along and bumps into him, no matter how hot-tempered the man may be, he will not get angry. But if there should be someone in the other boat, then he will shout out to haul this way or veer that. If his first shout is unheeded, he will shout again, and if that is not heard, he will shout a third time, this time with a torrent of curses following. In the first instance, he wasn't angry; now in the second he is. Earlier he faced emptiness, now he faces occupancy. If a man could succeed in making himself empty, and in that way wander through the world, then who could do him harm? [212]

Finally, when emotions cannot be avoided, man must evade the pain that accrues from their increasing inner tension by releasing them at once:

Mark what I say! . . . In the case of the emotions, it is best to let them follow where they will . . . By letting the emotions follow as they will, you avoid fatigue. [216]

Thus, the *Chuang Tzu* makes a clear distinction between conflicting feelings that man must endeavor to harmonize and emotions that he must avoid at all costs.

4. Pain-Avoidance on the Plane of Will Psychology:
A Rankian Interpretation

k. Eleventh Problem:

Pain of the Contradiction of Will and Counterwill

Diagram V shows that man's consciousness acts on Reality (man's mental representation of his world) by means of the will. Since man's consciousness is man's mental instrument of survival in his world, the will can be visualized as the cutting edge of such an instrument. For this reason, it is not surprising to see that the *Chuang Tzu* compares the will to a sword: "There is no weapon more deadly than the will — even Mo-yeh [the fabled sword of antiquity] is inferior to it." [255—56]

Diagram V also shows that, on the plane of Reality, pleasure is the affirmation of the will on Reality, at Point B, and that pain is the result of the repulsion of the will by Reality, at Point C of the diagram. The repulsion of the will by Reality (man's mental representation of his world) can be the result of either an objective situation or of a subjective situation. The repulsion of the will by Reality may be the result of an objective situation when man's will and action encounter obstacles in man's world. In this case, the solution to the problem of pain-avoidance demands an intelligent avoidance or circumvention of these obstacles, or as *Chuang Tzu* puts it: "To see that external things do not blunt the will is called perfection." [127] But the repulsion of the will by Reality may also be the result of a subjective situation when man's consciousness opposes man's will and action, as potential causes of trouble and, therefore, of pain. In this case, the solution to the problem of pain-avoidance demands that man's consciousness not interfere with man's will, or as the *Chuang Tzu* has it: "Do not hobble your will, or you will be departing far from the Way!" [181] In both cases, namely, in the objective and subjective repulsion of the will by Reality, mental pain occurs because the will to action is thwarted. More precisely, Diagram V above shows that mental pain occurs, at Point C of the diagram, because the will is split into two opposed wills, namely, into will to action (upper prong of the diagram), and counterwill to action (lower prong of the diagram). Accordingly, in both cases the solution to the problem of pain-avoidance on the plane of will psychology demands the unification of the dichotomized will into a single will. As the *Chuang Tzu* enjoins: "Make your will one!" [57]

The unification of the dichotomized will into a single will can be the result of three choices. First, it can be the result of the unification of the will into a single will to action that would be undeterred by any obstacles. According to the *Chuang Tzu*, such a solution is not acceptable, because the unification of the will into a single will to action would force man to act all the time and, as a result, would cause him fatigue, wear and tear, and pain. In other words, the *Chuang Tzu* condemns the unification of the will into a single will to action as the cause of the painful, compulsive neurosis:

In sleep, men's spirits go visiting; in waking hours, their bodies hustle. With everything they meet they become entangled. Day after day they use their minds in strife, sometimes grandiose, sometimes sly, sometimes petty. Their little fears are mean and trembly; their great fears are stunned and overwhelming. They bound off like an arrow or a crossbow pellet, certain that they are the arbiters of right and wrong. They cling to their position as though they had sworn before the gods, sure that they are holding on to victory. They fade like fall and winter — such is the way they dwindle day by day. They drown in what they do — you cannot make them turn back. They grow dark, as though sealed with seals — such are the excesses of their old age. And when their minds draw near to death, nothing can restore them to the light. [37]

Second, the unification of the dichotomized will into a single will can be the result of its unification into a single counterwill to action. In this case, will becomes a single will not to will. According to the *Chuang Tzu*, since man participates in life and, therefore, lives through willed action, the unification of the will into a single counterwill to action (the will not to will) is refusal to participate in life and refusal of life. Such a refusal creates the painful mental state of what we would call today, plain neurosis:

To be constrained in will, lofty in action [i.e. scorning action], aloof from the world, apart from its customs, elevated in discourse, sullen and critical, indignation his whole concern — such is the life favored by the scholar in his mountain valley, the man who condemns the world, the worn and haggard one who means to end it all with a plunge into the deep. [167]

Third and last, the unification of the will can be the result of the reconciliation, or harmonization, of will to action and counterwill to action. Since Reality consciousness is the vehicle of will to action, and Self-consciousness is the vehicle of the counterwill to action, such a reconciliation, or harmonization, of will and counterwill is also the reconciliation, or harmonization, of Reality consciousness and of Self-consciousness. And, as explained in the preceding chapter, the reconciliation, or harmonization, of Reality consciousness and of Self-consciousness is the means to avoid mental pain and to obtain mental pleasure. Consequently, the reconciliation, or harmonization, of will to action and counterwill to action banishes mental pain and produces mental pleasure on the plane of will psychology: ". . . to attain loftiness without constraining the will [i.e. without reducing the will to either will to action or counterwill to action] — this is the Way . . . of the sage." [168]

On the plane of Reality, mental pain is the result of man's consciousness of the resistance of Reality (man's mental representation of his world) to man's will to action. Indeed, Diagram V above shows that the resistance of Reality to will to action produces pain, at Point C of the diagram. Such a resistance of Reality to will to action can either be objective, whenever Reality stands as obstacle to man's action, or subjective, whenever man's action does not express man's "inborn nature," that is to say, man's capacity, propensity and talents for such an action. But consciousness of the resistance of Reality to man's will to action is consciousness of the effort that the action requires. Consequently, mental pain is the result of either an objective or of a subjective effort.

l. Twelfth Problem:

Pain of Objective Effort

Since pain is the result of the resistance of Reality to will to action and since consciousness of the resistance of Reality to will to action is consciousness of the effort that the action requires, the greater the effort, the greater the resultant mental pain. Accordingly, the solution to the problem of pain-avoidance, on the plane of will to action and Reality, is the achievement of an effortless action that the *Chuang Tzu* calls "inactive action":

> If he who launches into action is not really acting [i.e. doesn't furnish any effort], then his action is a launching into inaction. [260] To spend little effort and achieve big results – that is the Way of the sage. [135] So it is said, He who practices the Way [i.e. seeks pain-avoidance] does less every day, does less and goes on doing less, until he reaches the point where he does nothing, does nothing and yet there is nothing that is not done. [235] Thus it is that the Perfect Man does not act, the Great Sage does not move – they have perceived [the Way of] Heaven and earth, we may say. [236]

In the case of an objective effort, that is to say, when Reality (man's mental representation of his world) offers real obstacles to action, such an effortless, "inactive action" consists of circumventing these obstacles. Thus, effortless, "inactive action" demands an intelligent utilization of any situation in the outside world for the purpose of achieving an action that would not meet with any resistance on the part of the world and that, consequently, would not cause any mental pain:

> With inaction, you may make the world work for you and have leisure to spare; with action, you will find yourself working for the world and never will it be enough. [144]

m. Thirteenth Problem:

Pain of Subjective Effort

As explained above, the subjective effort that causes mental pain is the consciousness of the fact that man's action goes against the grain of man's "inborn nature":

> The inborn nature is the substance of life. The inborn nature in motion is called action. Action which has become artificial [i.e. which is no longer the expression of the inborn nature] is called loss. [259]

By "inborn nature" the *Chuang Tzu* means "individual characteristics and limitations" of the "forms and bodies." [131–132] More precisely, such an "inborn nature" manifests itself in individual talents, function, skill and nature of all created things:

> The little hens of Yüeh cannot hatch goose eggs, though the larger hens of Lu can do it well enough. It isn't that one kind of hen isn't just as henlike as the other. One can and the other can't because their talents just naturally differ in size. [251] A beam or pillar can be used to batter down a city wall, but it is no good for stopping up a little hole – this refers to a difference in function. Thoroughbreds like Ch'i-chi and Hua-liu could gallop a thousand li in one day, but when it came to catching rats they were no match for the wildcat or the weasel – this refers to a difference in skill. The horned owl catches fleas at night and can spot the tip of a hair, but when daylight comes, no matter how wide it opens its eyes, it cannot see a mound or a hill – this refers to a difference in nature. [180]

Thus, in order to avoid the mental pain that results from subjective effort, man must, first of all, act in accordance with his inborn nature. For any action that does not express man's inborn nature is insincere and, as such, is bound to end in failure: "If you do not perceive the sincerity within yourself and yet try to move forth, each movement will miss the mark." [255] Since failed action is a cause of mental pain, the pursuit of pain-avoidance demands a thorough knowledge of the scope and limitation of one's inborn nature for the successful choice and performance of one's action:

The wind said, "It's true that I whirl up from the North Sea and whirl off to the South Sea. But if you hold up a finger against me you've defeated me, and if you trample on me you've likewise defeated me. On the other hand, I can break down big trees and blow over great houses – this is a talent that I alone have. So I take all the mass of little defeats and make them into a Great Victory. To make a Great Victory – only the sage is capable of that!" [184]

n. Fourteenth Problem:

Pain of Consciousness on the Plane of Will Psychology.
The Subconscious Mind and Subconscious, Conditioned Reflexes.

As Diagram V above shows, Self-consciousness is the vehicle of the will that has been repulsed by Reality, or simply, that Self-consciousness is the vehicle of the counterwill. Consequently, excessive Self-consciousness represents a strong counterwill that is capable of frustrating will to action and of causing mental pain on the plane of will psychology. It stands, therefore, to reason that, in order to avoid the mental pain that Self-consciousness causes on the plane of the will, man's consciousness must deny Self-consciousness, that is to say, deny the Self. Illustrating this point, the *Chuang Tzu* presents an interview between Confucius and a fearless swimmer, who swam in the midst of a dangerous torrent. In this interview, Confucius asked the swimmer how he could swim in such dangerous waters without fear for his life. To this the swimmer replied:

"I have no way. I began with what I was used to, grew up with my nature, and let things come to completion with fate. I go under with the swirls and come out with the eddies, following along the way the water goes and never thinking about myself. That's how I can stay afloat." [205]

But Diagram V also describes the fact that Self-consciousness is the direct result of the repulsion of Reality consciousness by Reality. This means that, in order to deny Self-consciousness, as cause of mental pain on the plane of will psychology, man's consciousness must also deny Reality consciousness, that is to say, deny Reality:

> Confucius said, "A good swimmer will in no time get the knack of it — that means he's forgotten the water [i.e. Reality]." [200] If outside concerns enter and are not expelled [i.e. denied], each movement will only add failure to failure. [255]

Thus, in order to put an end to the mental pain that Self-consciousness causes on the plane of will psychology, man's consciousness must deny both the Self and Reality. But, as explained in the preceding chapter, the denial of both the Self and Reality is the "emptying of the mind" that is a precondition for the substitution of the conscious mind by the subconscious mind. Accordingly, on the plane of will to action, denial of the Self and Reality is a precondition for the substitution of the consciously willed action by subconscious action. Moreover, just as in the case of the substitution of the conscious mind by the subconscious mind, the substitution of the consciously willed action by subconscious action must be induced whenever needed. Thus, the *Chuang Tzu* recommends a timely cooperation between subconscious action and consciously willed action:

> Action which is done because one cannot do otherwise [i.e. subconscious action] is called virtue. Action in which there is nothing other than self [i.e. consciously willed action] is called good order. In definition the two seem to be opposites but in reality they agree. [259]

According to the *Chuang Tzu*, in order to achieve its goal, subconscious action must be equal or superior to its task. To this effect, subconscious action must be the expression of both man's inborn nature and of a long and good training. For this reason, in order to be efficient, subconscious action must be the result of conditioned reflexes. Consequently, the timely cooperation between subconscious action and consciously willed action is a cooperation between subconscious, conditioned reflexes and consciously willed action. The parable of Cook Ting illustrates this point:

Cook Ting was cutting up an ox for Lord Wen-hui. At every touch of his hand, every heave of his shoulder, every move of his feet, every thrust of his knee — zip! zoop! He slithered the knife along with a zing, and all was in perfect rhythm, as though he were performing the dance of the Mulberry Grove or keeping time to the Ching-shou music.

"Ah, this is marvelous!" said Lord Wen-hui. "Imagine skill reaching such height!"

Cook Ting laid down his knife and replied, "What I care about is the Way [i.e. pain-avoidance], which goes beyond skill. When I first began cutting up oxen, all I could see was the ox itself. After three years I no longer saw the whole ox. And now — now I go at it by spirit [i.e. subconscious mind] and don't look with my eyes [i.e. consciously]. Perception and understanding have come to a stop and spirit [the subconscious mind] moves where it wants. I go along with the natural makeup, strike in the big hollows, guide the knife through the big openings, and follow things as they are [and thus avoid all effort]. So I never touch the smallest ligament or tendon, much less a main joint."

"A good cook changes his knife once a year — because he cuts. A mediocre cook changes his knife once a month — because he hacks. I've had this knife of mine for nineteen years and I've cut up thousands of oxen with it, and yet the blade is as good as though it had just come from the grindstone. There are spaces between the joints, and the blade of the knife has really no thickness. If you insert what has no thickness into such spaces, then there's plenty of room — more than enough for the blade to play about in. That's why after nineteen years the blade of my knife is still as good as when it first came from the grindstone."

"However, whenever I come to a complicated place, I size up the difficulties, tell myself to watch out and be careful, keep my eyes on what I'm doing, work very slowly, and move the knife with the greatest subtlety [i.e. I act consciously], until — flop! the whole thing comes apart like a clod of earth crumbling to the ground. I stand there holding the knife and look all around me, completely satisfied and reluctant to move on, and then I wipe off the knife and put it away."

"Excellent!" said Lord Wen-hui. "I have heard the words of Cook Ting and learned how to care for life!" [50–51]

Pain of Opposition of Individual Will to Social Will

When Reality is man's mental representation of his social world, the repulsion of man's will to action by Reality is the repulsion of man's individual will by the will of his social world. In this case, the painful opposition of will to action and counterwill to action is the painful opposition of man's will to action to the will of his social world. Ostensibly, in order to avoid the pain of such an opposition, man can do three things: (1) He can bring his will into conformity with the will of his social world; (2) He can deny the will of his social world by imposing and asserting his own individual will; (3) Lastly, he can bring into harmony his individual will with the will of his social world. According to the *Chuang Tzu*, these three ostensible solutions to the problem of the avoidance of pain that results from the opposition of man's individual will to the will of his social world are false solutions, because they are all sources of mental pain. Indeed, as explained above, since the will is the agent of the Ego on the plane of Reality, the conformity of the individual will with the will of the social world injures the individuality of the Ego and, as such, causes mental pain. Similarly, the imposition and assertion of the will against the will of the social world injure the sociability of the Ego and, as such, also cause mental pain. For these reasons, both the conformity and the imposition and assertion of the will must be rejected: "A will that takes refuge in conformity, behavior that is aloof and eccentric — neither of these, alas, is compatible with perfect wisdom and solid virtue." [299]

The rejection of the third ostensible solution to the problem of the avoidance of pain that results from the confrontation of man's individual will with the will of his social world is not so immediately obvious. Indeed, as explained above, the solution to the problem of pain-avoidance on the plane of will psychology requires a harmonization of will and counterwill; in this case, a harmonization of man's individual will with the will of man's social world. And such a harmonization can only mean acceptance of man's individual will by his social world. It also means that the goals that man's individual will pursues must be socially acceptable goals. According to the *Chuang Tzu*, these socially acceptable goals are reputation or fame and gain or wealth:

> After all, there are no men who do not strive for reputation and seek gain. If you're rich, people flock to you; flocking to you, they bow and scrape; and when they bow and scrape, this shows they honor you. To have men bowing and scraping, offering you honor – this is the way to insure length of years, ease to the body, joy to the will. [335]

But the possession of fame and wealth generates the painful fear of losing them:

> He who considers wealth a good thing can never bear to give up his income; he who considers eminence a good thing can never bear to give up his fame. He who has a taste for power can never bear to hand over authority to others. Holding tight to these things, such men shiver with fear; should they let them go, they would pine in sorrow. They never stop for a moment of reflection, never cease to gaze with greedy eyes – they are men punished by Heaven. [162]

On the other hand, failure to achieve the socially acceptable goals of one's individual will is also the cause of mental pain, for such a failure is the defeat of one's will to action by social Reality. In other words, both success and failure in the pursuit of the socially acceptable goals of one's individual will cause pain: "If you do succeed, you are bound to suffer from the yin and yang. If you do not succeed, you are bound to suffer from the judgment of men." [59]

Thus, a harmonization of man's individual will with the will of his social world by means of the pursuit of fame and wealth causes mental pain, and as such it is a false solution to the problem of pain-avoidance on the plane of the confrontation of man's individual will with the will of his social world. Indeed, for the *Chuang Tzu*, recognition, eminence, authority, profit, fame and wealth – the so-called socially acceptable goals are nothing but the delusions of the will:

Wipe out the delusions of the will . . . open up the roadblocks in the Way. Eminence and wealth, recognition and authority, fame and profit — these six are the delusions of the will. [259] Therefore he who sets his eyes on reputation will find that it is nowhere to be seen; he who seeks for gain will find that it is not to be gotten. To entrap the mind and the body in a scramble for such things — is this not delusion indeed? [338]

Since the will is the agent of the Ego/Self, the pursuit of the socially acceptable goals of fame and wealth is not only a sixfold delusion of the will but also a sixfold delusion of the Ego/Self. Consequently, in order to avoid the pain of the fear of loss of fame and wealth that results from such a pursuit (see above), the follower of the Way must simultaneously deny the value of fame and wealth and deny his Ego/Self. In other words, the follower of the Way must "empty his mind" of both Reality (fame and wealth) and the Ego/Self:

The Man of the Way wins no fame, the highest virtue wins no gain, the Great Man has no self. [179] Being selfless, how then can he look upon possession as possession? . . . He who fixes his eyes on nothingness [i.e. he who has an "empty mind"] — he is the true friend of Heaven and earth. [124] Vacant, addled, he seems close to madness [i.e. in the eyes of others]. Wiping out his footprints, sloughing off his power [i.e. ridding himself of the Self, the Ego and will], he does not work for success or fame. So he has no cause to blame other men [for opposing his will], nor other men to blame him [for his will]. [214] Hence he who nourishes his will forgets about his bodily form [and thus endangers it]; he who nourishes his bodily form [i.e. he who seeks to avoid pain] forgets about questions of gain; and he who arrives at the Way forgets about his mind. [317]

p. Sixteenth Problem:

Pain of Success and Pain of Failure. Self-Determination and Fate.

This sixteenth and last problem of pain-avoidance is a corollary to the preceding one. Indeed, Diagram V above shows that pleasure occurs when the will asserts itself on Reality, at Point B of the diagram, and that pain occurs when Reality repulses the will, at Point C of the diagram. This means that the success of the will is a cause of mental pleasure and that the failure of the will is a cause of mental pain. When the will seeks to achieve the socially acceptable goals of fame and wealth, the pleasurable success of the will is attainment of fame and wealth. Conversely, the painful failure of the will is failure to achieve fame and wealth. But, as explained above, the achievement of fame and wealth, that is to say, success of the will, is the cause of subsequent mental pain. Thus, both the success of the will and the failure of the will are causes of mental pain. According to the *Chuang Tzu*, avoidance of the pain that results from the success of the will demands the denial of the pursuit of success:

> I have heard the Man of Great Completion say: "Boasts are a sign of no success; success once won faces overthrow; fame once won faces ruin." Who can rid himself of success and fame, return and join the common run of men? [214]

In turn, he who does not pursue success cannot fail and, therefore, cannot suffer the pain of failure.

But, more generally, man must will in order to survive. In this case, the failure of the will is a threat to man's survival, and as such, it is a cause of mental pain that one could call fear of death. According to the *Chuang Tzu*, in order to avoid the mental pain that accrues from the failure of the will to survive, man must give up his painful will and surrender to the unavoidable, that is, to Fate:

> To know what you can't do anything about, and to be content with it as you would with fate — only a man of virtue can do that. [70] Just go along with things and let your mind move freely. Resign yourself to what cannot be avoided and nourish what is within you [i.e. take care of your mind] — this is best. What more do you have to do to fulfill your mission [i.e. pain-avoidance]? Nothing is as good as following orders (obeying fate) — that's how difficult it is! [61]

In contradistinction to surrender to Fate, man's will to survive is man's will to self-determination. Since man must will in order to survive, surrender to Fate is a corrective to the failure of the will to self-determination. Indeed, the *Chuang Tzu* urges the follower of the Way to pursue self-determination, but fall back on Fate whenever self-determination fails. For this reason, self-determination must never eliminate the notion of Fate: "So I say: do not let what is human [i.e. will to self-determination] wipe out what is Heavenly [i.e. Fate]; do not let what is purposeful [i.e. self-determination] wipe out what is fated . . ." [183]

Finally, since self-determination is assertion of the Self on Reality by means of the will, denial of the will to self-determination is also a denial of the Self and of Reality, as subject and object of self-determination. And, since the Self and Reality represent the notion of earth, submission to pain-freeing Fate through denial of the Self and Reality is submission to the Way of Heaven which, as the Natural Law of the universe, is responsible for everything in the world. Consequently, he who denies his painful will to self-determination and submits to Fate joins the Way of Heaven and experiences Heavenly joy (see Chapter One):

> Confucius said, "Life, death, preservation, loss, failure, success, poverty, riches, worthiness, unworthiness, slander, fame, hunger, thirst, cold, heat − these are the alternations of the world, the workings of fate . . . If you can harmonize and delight in them, master them and never be at a loss for joy, if you can do this day and night without break and make it be spring [i.e. the season of joy] with everything, mingling with all and creating the moment within your own mind − this is what I call being whole in power." [73−74]

This chapter has presented the *Chuang Tzu's* sixteen problems of pain-avoidance on the planes of the psychologies of the Ego, feeling and emotions, will and action, as well as their solutions. Of the sixteen solutions to these problems of pain-avoidance, two are prohibitions (Tenth and Fifteenth Problem), two are utilization of one's world and of one's limitations (Twelfth and Thirteenth Problems), and twelve of them demand the harmonization of opposites.

It is, therefore, possible to say that the predominant mode of the solutions to the problems of pain-avoidance on the planes of the psychologies of the Ego, feeling and emotions, will and action is harmonization of opposites. This does not come as a surprise for these psychological opposites are the result of the dichotomy of man's consciousness into a dialectical opposition of Reality consciousness and Self-consciousness to one another. And, as explained in the preceding chapter, mental pain is the result of the dialectical opposition of Reality consciousness and Self-consciousness, while absence of mental pain and pleasure are the result of their reconciliation, or harmony.

Chapter Three

PAIN-AVOIDANCE ON THE PLANE OF KNOWLEDGE AS INTELLECT: CONSCIOUS SIMPLE APPREHENSION, SUBCONSCIOUS KNOWLEDGE, OR INTUITION, AND GREAT WISDOM, OR INSTINCT. CONSCIOUS KNOWLEDGE AND THE FALL OF MANKIND. A TAOIST UTOPIA

1. Conscious Simple Apprehension

The upper prong of Diagram V (p. 63) shows that knowledge converts painful feeling into pleasurable will, and the lower prong of the diagram shows that knowledge converts painful will into pleasurable feeling. This means that knowledge is the conscious instrument of pain-avoidance and of pursuit of pleasure of man's consciousness. But Diagram V also shows that knowledge is the result of painful feeling and of painful will and, as such, is painful knowledge. Consequently, in order to be the conscious instrument of pain-avoidance and of the pursuit of pleasure, knowledge must have a core that would be free from and independent of painful feeling and painful will. Such a core of knowledge is the intellect which, by definition, is knowledge that is free from individual feeling and individual will. It is, therefore, possible to qualify Diagram V by saying that it is the intellect that is the conscious instrument of pain-avoidance and of pursuit of pleasure of man's consciousness.

As explained in Chapter One, pain-avoidance and pursuit of pleasure demand that the Self (man's mental representation of himself) and Reality (man's mental representation of his world) be experienced as parts of a greater whole. Consequently, as the conscious instrument of pain-avoidance and of pursuit of pleasure, the intellect is the part of man's consciousness that establishes the relation between the knowledge of the Self and of Reality, as parts, with the notion of their greater whole. Again, as explained in Chapter One, the relation between the notion of parts and whole is dialectical and cyclical. Accordingly, the intellect is the part of man's consciousness that establishes a dialectical and cyclical relation between the knowledge of the Self and of Reality, as parts, with the notion of their greater whole. Lastly, as explained in Chapter One, since in its utmost expression it represents man's total terrestrial experience, the relation between the Self and Reality, as parts, can be encapsulated in the notion of earth (parts = the Self and Reality); in this case, the notion of their greater whole is the notion of Heaven (whole). But knowledge of the Self and Reality, as parts, is knowledge of man's consciousness, or human knowledge. Therefore, in its utmost expression, the intellect is the part of man's consciousness that establishes the dialectical and cyclical relation between human knowledge and the knowledge of Heaven, or Heavenly knowledge. Again, since human knowledge is knowledge of parts (the Self and Reality) and Heavenly knowledge is knowledge of the whole, and, since parts and whole are both the cause and the result of one another (see Chapter One), such a dialectical and cyclical relation means that human knowledge complements Heavenly knowledge and that Heavenly knowledge complements human knowledge. According to the *Chuang Tzu*, such a mutual completion of human knowledge and of Heavenly knowledge is "true knowledge" or "perfection of knowledge":

> There must first be a True Man before there can be true knowledge. What do I mean by a True Man?* [77] When man and Heaven do not defeat each other [but complement one another], then we may be said to have the True Man. [80] He who knows what it is that Heaven does, and knows what it is that man does, has reached the peak. Knowing what it is that Heaven does, he lives with Heaven. Knowing what it is that man does, he uses the knowledge of what he knows to help out the knowledge of what he doesn't know, and lives out the years that Heaven gave him without being cut off midway — this is the perfection of knowledge. [77]

---

* *The Complete Works of Chuang Tzu*, translated by Burton Watson (Columbia University Press, New York and London, 1968). Throughout the chapter, the page-number of the quotation is indicated in the square brackets that follow the quotation.

As knowledge of parts (the Self and Reality) of the greater whole of Heaven, human knowledge is also knowledge of the eight attributes of the notion of parts (see Chapter One), namely, knowledge of form, of limitation in space and time, of being, of life, of liveliness (fullness, motivity, turbidity, noise, and action), of multiplicity, of diversity, and of name. But such a knowledge can only be the product of sensorial perceptions. Consequently, as knowledge of parts (the Self and Reality) of the greater whole of Heaven, human knowledge is perceptual knowledge.

Similarly, as knowledge of the whole, knowledge of Heaven, or Heavenly knowledge, is also the knowledge of the eight attributes of the notion of whole (see Chapter One), namely, knowledge of formlessness, of nonlimitation in space and time, of nonbeing, of death, of tranquility (emptiness, stillness, limpidity, silence, and inaction), of oneness, of sameness, and of namelessness. Such a knowledge is conceptual knowledge. Consequently, as knowledge of the whole, knowledge of Heaven, or Heavenly knowledge, is conceptual knowledge.

Thus, as cycle of transformation of the dialectically opposed human knowledge (knowledge of parts) and of Heavenly knowledge (knowledge of the whole) into one another, "true knowledge," or "perfection of knowledge," is a cycle of transformation of the dialectically opposed perceptual knowledge (knowledge of parts) and conceptual knowledge (knowledge of the whole) into one another. But, as any student of logic knows, the cyclical transformation of knowledge of parts (perceptual knowledge) and knowledge of the whole (conceptual knowledge) into one another is called the process of simple apprehension. Indeed, the process of simple apprehension is the process of the completion of knowledge of parts and of knowledge of the whole by one another. More precisely, since the transition from the knowledge of parts (perceptual knowledge) to the knowledge of the whole (conceptual knowledge) is induction and the transition from knowledge of the whole (conceptual knowledge) to the knowledge of parts (perceptual knowledge) is deduction, the "true knowledge," or "perfection of knowledge," of the *Chuang Tzu* can be described by the following diagram of simple apprehension:

Diagram VI: Structure of Simple Apprehension
("True Knowledge" or "Perfection of Knowledge")

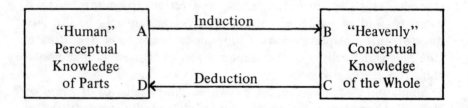

This diagram describes the cooperation between the "human," perceptual knowledge (knowledge of parts) and the "Heavenly," conceptual knowledge (knowledge of the whole). According to the *Chuang Tzu*, since it is the product of the sensorial perception of phenomena that take place in man's world, "human," perceptual knowledge (knowledge of parts) is knowledge of the world and, as such, is "outer knowledge." Similarly, since it is the product of the intellect, "Heavenly," conceptual knowledge (knowledge of the whole) is "inner knowledge": "Hence, it is said: the Heavenly is on the inside, the human is on the outside." [182] Consequently, the cooperation between the "human," perceptual knowledge (knowledge of parts) and the "Heavenly," conceptual knowledge (knowledge of the whole), as described in Diagram VI above, is a cooperation between "outer knowledge" (i.e. perceptual knowledge) and "inner knowledge" (i.e. conceptual knowledge). As the *Chuang Tzu* puts it:

Let your ears and eyes [perceptual knowledge] communicate with what is inside [conceptual knowledge], and put mind and knowledge [conceptual knowledge] on the outside. Then even gods and spirits will come to dwell, not to speak of men! [58] Therefore, when things enter [the sage's] mind from the outside [i.e. perceptual knowledge], there is a host [i.e. "inner," conceptual knowledge] to receive them but not to cling to them; and when things come forth from his mind [i.e. from the "inner," conceptual knowledge], there is a mark [i.e. perceptual knowledge] to guide them but not to constrain them. [290]

Such a cooperation between the "outer," "human," perceptual knowledge and the "inner," "Heavenly," conceptual knowledge is indispensable to "true knowledge," or "perfection of knowledge," for without the cooperation of "Heavenly," conceptual knowledge, knowledge reduces itself to perceptual knowledge, that is to say, to a mere sensorial knowledge. But, since different senses convey different perceptions to the mind, such a sensorial, perceptual knowledge is a confused tangle of different sensorial perceptions:

> . . . it is like the case of the ear, the eye, the nose, and the mouth: each has its own kind of understanding, but their functions are not interchangeable. [364] If the mind does not have its Heavenly wanderings [i.e. conceptual knowledge], then the six apertures of sensation [the ears, the eyes, the nose, and the mouth] will defeat each other. [301]

Conversely, without the cooperation of "outer," "human," "perceptual knowledge, knowledge reduces itself to conceptual knowledge, that is to say, to baseless intellection. Such a knowledge is only capable of putting forth unverified notions and, for this reason, is not and cannot be true knowledge. Consequently, in its quest for "true knowledge," or "perfection of knowledge," the sage follower of the Way must reject knowledge that is the single product of either "outer," perceptual knowledge or "inner," conceptual knowledge:

> If there is no host on the inside [i.e. conceptual knowledge] to receive it, it [perceptual knowledge] will not stay; if there is no mark on the outside [i.e. perceptual knowledge] to guide it [the conceptual knowledge], it will not go. If what is brought forth from the inside [i.e. conceptual knowledge] is not received on the outside [i.e. by perceptual knowledge], then the sage will not bring it forth. If what is taken in from the outside [i.e. perceptual knowledge] is not received by a host on the inside [i.e. by conceptual knowledge], the sage will not entrust it. [161]

According to the *Chuang Tzu*, all knowledge that accrues from the cooperation of "outer," "human," perceptual knowledge (knowledge of parts) with "inner," "Heavenly," conceptual knowledge (knowledge of the whole) must be verified by a valid experience:

> The torch of chaos and doubt — this is what the sage steers by. So he does not use things but relegates all to the constant. This is what it means to use clarity. [42] The constant is the useful [i.e. valid]; the useful [i.e. the valid] is the passable [i.e. the acceptable]; the passable [i.e. the acceptable] is the successful; and with success, all is accomplished. He relies upon this alone, relies upon it and does not know he is doing so. This is called the Way. [41]

For the *Chuang Tzu*, a valid experience is an experience that must reproduce a situation, as it exists in life. Indeed, the cooperation between perceptual knowledge (knowledge of parts) and conceptual knowledge (knowledge of the whole) is the relation that exists between analysis and synthesis. And synthesis, for the *Chuang Tzu*, is the re-creation of the integrity of the whole, grasped as a living entity. More precisely, since perceptual knowledge is knowledge of parts, it is the product of the analysis of the whole. On the other hand, conceptual knowledge is knowledge of the whole; as such, it is the product of the synthesis of parts. Consequently simple apprehension ("true knowledge" or "perfection of knowledge") is a cycle of analysis (knowledge of parts) and synthesis (knowledge of the whole). Moreover, according to the *Chuang Tzu*, the notion of the whole is the notion of the organic unity of its parts, as living entity. As such, the notion of the organic whole is different from and superior to the notion of the sum of its component parts:

> The hundred joints, the nine openings, the six organs, all come together and exist here [as my body]. But which part should I feel closest to? I should delight in all parts, you say? But there must be one I ought to favor more. If not, are they all of them mere servants? But if they are all servants, then how can they keep order among themselves? Or do they take turns being lord and servant? It would seem as though there must be some True Lord among them [the notion of the whole]. But whether I succeed in discovering his identity or not, it neither adds to nor detracts from his Truth. [38]

Since the notion of the whole is the notion of the organic unity of its parts, as living entity, each and every part of the whole has a vital significance that can only be grasped from its relation to the living whole:

> Out of the murk, things come to life. With cunning you declare, "We must analyze this!" You try putting your analysis in words . . . You cannot, however, attain understanding. At the winter sacrifice, you can point to the tripe or the hoof of the sacrificial ox, which can be considered separate things, and yet in a sense cannot be considered separate [because they are parts of the living entity of the ox]. [258]

Again, since the notion of the whole is the notion of the living whole, analysis (knowledge of parts) without synthesis (knowledge of the living whole) is a fragmentation and a destruction of the living whole into dead parts. As such, analysis without synthesis is knowledge of the death of the living whole. And, since fear of death causes mental pain, analysis without synthesis is a knowledge of death that increases man's fear of death and its resultant mental pain. For this reason, analysis without synthesis is a danger to man's mental health:

> The Way permeates all things. Their dividedness is their completeness, their completeness is their impairment. What is hateful about this state of dividedness is that men take their dividedness and seek to supplement it [with analysis]; and what is hateful about attempts to supplement it is that they are a mere supplementation of what men already have. So they go forth [into analysis] and forget to return [to the notion of the living whole] — they act as though they had seen a ghost. They go forth [into analysis] and claim to have gotten something — what they have gotten is the thing called death. They are wiped out and chocked off — already a kind of ghost themselves. [256]

Lastly, since analysis without synthesis yields knowledge of the dead parts of the living whole, analytical knowledge is spurious knowledge, for it is not a knowledge of things, as they exist in real life. By the same token, since synthesis yields knowledge of the living whole, synthetic knowledge is true knowledge, and as such, it is far superior to the spurious analytical knowledge:

> So [I say,] those who divide [i.e. analyze] fail to divide [i.e. fail to know the parts of the whole]; those who discriminate fail to discriminate. What does this mean, you ask? The sage embraces things [i.e. the sage has recourse to synthesis]. Ordinary men discriminate among them [i.e. analyze things] and parade their discriminations [as if they were truths] before others. So I say, those who discriminate [i.e. analyze] fail to see. [44]

From what has just been presented, it is clear that the Philosophy of the Way, or Taoism, of the *Chuang Tzu* is anchored in an organic worldview, where synthesis is always superior to analysis, because it produces the knowledge of things, as living entities, or organisms.

2. Conversion of the Eight Cycles of the Way into Cycles of Simple Apprehension (Perfection of Knowledge)

As explained in Chapter One, the eight cycles of the Way of Heaven and earth are also the eight cycles of the dialectical opposition of the notions of parts and whole to one another. Since perceptual knowledge is knowledge of parts and conceptual knowledge is knowledge of the whole, the relation between perceptual knowledge and conceptual knowledge is expressed by the eight cycles of the dialectical opposition of the notions of parts and whole to one another and of the Way. Thus, the eight cycles of the Way are also the eight cycles of simple apprehension, as dialectical opposition of perceptual knowledge (knowledge of parts) and conceptual knowledge (knowledge of the whole) to one another. But these eight cycles, namely: Form ⇌ Formlessness; Limitation in Space and Time ⇌ Nonlimitation in Space and Time; Being ⇌ Nonbeing; Life ⇌ Death; Liveliness (fullness, motivity, turbidity, noise, and action) ⇌ Tranquility (emptiness, stillness, limpidity, silence and inaction); Multiplicity ⇌ Oneness; Diversity ⇌ Sameness; and Name ⇌ Namelessness, do not represent any recognizable, cognitive attributes. It is, therefore, necessary to show how the *Chuang Tzu* converts these eight cycles of the Way into cycles that adequately describe the process of simple apprehension.

a. Form ⇌ Formlessness = Formal Knowledge ⇌ Imagination

As explained in Chapter One, the first attribute of the notion of parts is form. Consequently, as knowledge of parts, perceptual knowledge is knowledge of form, or formal knowledge. Again, the first attribute of the notion of the whole, as the dialectical opposite of the notion of parts, is formlessness. Consequently, as knowledge of the whole, conceptual knowledge is knowledge of formlessness, and as such it is nonformal knowledge, or imaginative knowledge. Thus, the relation between perceptual knowledge (knowledge of parts) and conceptual knowledge (knowledge of the whole) that forms simple apprehension (perfection of knowledge) can be described by the following equation:

Simple Apprehension (Perfection of Knowledge) = Perceptual Knowledge (Knowledge of Parts) ⇌ Conceptual Knowledge (Knowledge of the Whole) = Form ⇌ Formlessness (First Cycle of the Way and of Simple Apprehension) = Formal Knowledge ⇌ Imagination.

Indeed, simple apprehension (perfection of knowledge) demands that "formless" or "shapeless" imagination supplement formal knowledge:

The Yellow Emperor sent Knowledge [i.e. formal knowledge] to look for the Dark Pearl [i.e. the (hidden?) truth], but Knowledge couldn't find it. He sent the keen-eyed [i.e. perceptive] Li Chu to look for it, but Li Chu couldn't find it. He sent Wrangling Debate to look for it, but Wrangling Debate couldn't find it. At last he tried employing Shapeless [i.e. "formless" knowledge, or imagination], and Shapeless found it. [129]

As a matter of fact, the role of imagination is to expand and to enrich formal knowledge:

[Logician] Hui Tzu said to Chuang Tzu, "The king of Wei gave me some seeds of a huge gourd. I planted them, and when they grew up, the fruit was big enough to hold five piculs. I tried using it for a water container, but it was so heavy I couldn't lift it. I split it in half to make dippers, but they were so large and unwieldy that I couldn't dip them into anything. It's not that the gourds weren't fantastically big — but I decided they were of no use and so I smashed them to pieces."

Chuang Tzu said, "You certainly are dense when it comes to using big things! . . . Now you had a gourd big enough to hold five piculs. Why didn't you think of making it into a great tub so you could go floating around the rivers and lakes, instead of worrying because it was too big and unwieldy to dip into things! Obviously you still have a lot of underbrush in your head!" [34—35]

106

b. Limitation in Space and Time ⇌ Nonlimitation in Space and Time = Finite Knowledge ⇌ Infinite Knowledge

As explained in Chapter One, form is first and foremost limitation in space. Conversely, formlessness is nonlimitation in space. Consequently, the notion of nonlimited, or infinite, space is the product of the notion of formlessness. But the notion of formlessness is the product of the notion of form. Hence the notion of nonlimited, or infinite, space is the product of the notion of formlessness, which, in turn, is the product of the notion of form. According to the *Chuang Tzu*, there are two kinds of formlessness: First, the formlessness of a form that is so small as to have no form; second, the formlessness of a form that is so large that no form can encompass it. For this reason, the notion of nonlimited, or infinite, space is the mental representation of the expanse between the formless, infinitely small form and the formless, infinitely large form:

> The Lord of the River said, "Men who debate such matters these days all claim that the minutest thing has no form and the largest thing cannot be encompassed. Is this a true statement?"
> Jo of the North Sea said, "If from the standpoint of the minute we look at what is large, we cannot see to the end. If from the standpoint of what is large we look at what is minute, we cannot distinguish it clearly. The minute is the smallest of the small, the gigantic is the largest of the large, and it is therefore convenient to distinguish between them. [178]

Since, as explained in Chapter One, formlessness is the attribute of the notion of the greater whole of Heaven (sky), universal space is unlimited, or infinite space:

> Wavering heat, bits of dust, living things blowing each other about – the sky looks very blue. Is that its real color, or is it because it is so far away and has no end? [29]
> [Tai Chin-jen said,] . . . "Do you believe that there is a limit to the four directions [i.e. North, South, East and West], to up and down?"
> "They have no limits," said the ruler. [284]

Thus, in contradistinction to the Ptolemaic notion of finite space, the *Chuang Tzu's* notion of unlimited, or infinite, space is decidedly Copernican.

Again, as mentioned in Chapter One, the form exists as long as the thing that it defines and encompasses exists. For this reason, form represents the duration of the thing that it defines and encompasses and, as such, form represents limitation in time. Since the time of the existence of a thing is the past and present time, this limitation in time is past and present time. Conversely, formlessness is nonlimitation in time, and nonlimited, or infinite, time is a time that has no past and no present. But the very essence of time is its passage, its flow. To say, therefore, that nonlimited, or infinite, time has no past and no present and that it flows can only mean three things. First, since it has no past and no present, nonlimited, or infinite, time has no beginning (past) and no end (present). Second, since such a beginningless and endless time flows, nonlimited, or infinite, time is a cyclical time. Third and last, since it is a beginningless and endless cycle that has no past and no present, nonlimited, or infinite, time is a time where the present and the past are identical, that is to say, where the present repeats the past and the past repeats the present. Such a time is an eternally recurrent time (cf. Nietzsche's *ewige Wiederkehr*). Thus, nonlimited, or infinite, time is a cyclical time that has no past and no present, no beginning and no end, and is an eternally recurrent time:

> Jan Ch'iu asked Confucius, "Is it possible to know anything about the time before Heaven and earth existed?" [i.e. about the nonlimited, or infinite, time of formlessness].
> Confucius said, "It is — the past is the present." . . . "There is no past and no present, no beginning and no end. Sons and grandsons existed before sons and grandsons existed [i.e. nonlimited, or infinite, time is a recurrent time] — may we make such a statement?" [245] Past and present it has been the same; nothing can do injury to this [principle]. [101]

Since form is limitation in space and time and formlessness is nonlimitation in space and time, nonlimited, or infinite, time is coextensive with nonlimited, or infinite, space:

I look for the roots of the past, but they extend back and back without end. I search for the termination of the future, but it never stops coming at me. [293]

Lastly, since form is limitation in space and time, perceptual knowledge of form is a knowledge that is limited by space and time and, as such, is finite knowledge. Similarly, since formlessness is non-limitation in space and time, the perceptual knowledge of formlessness is knowledge that is not limited in space and time and, as such, is infinite knowledge. Thus, the relation between perceptual knowledge (knowledge of parts) and conceptual knowledge (knowledge of the whole) that forms simple apprehension (perfection of knowledge) can be expressed by the formula:

Simple Apprehension (Perfection of Knowledge) = Perceptual Knowledge (Knowledge of Parts) $\rightleftharpoons$ Conceptual Knowledge (Knowledge of the Whole) = Form $\rightleftharpoons$ Formlessness (First Cycle of the Way and of Simple Apprehension) = Limitation in Space and Time $\rightleftharpoons$ Nonlimitation in Space and Time (Second Cycle of the Way and of Simple Apprehension) = Finite Knowledge $\rightleftharpoons$ Infinite Knowledge.

As a corollary to the above, the *Chuang Tzu* rejects any and all teleological pursuit of the knowledge of primal and final causes. Since perceptual knowledge is sensorial knowledge of things, the time of perceptual knowledge is the present time of the sensorial experience. Consequently, perceptual knowledge cannot be knowledge of the past, primal causes, or of the future, final causes of things. But, as explained above, without the concrete evidence of perceptual knowledge, conceptual knowledge is unverifiable speculation. For this reason, as cycle of transformation and cooperation of perceptual knowledge and conceptual knowledge, simple apprehension (perfection of knowledge) cannot be a knowledge of primal or final causes of things. Accordingly, the pursuit of the Way on the plane of the intellect by means of simple apprehension (perfection of knowledge) demands the avoidance of the pursuit of primal and final causes of things:

. . . Chickens squawk, dogs bark — this is something men understand. But no matter how great their understanding, they cannot explain in words how the chicken and the dog have come to be what they are, nor can they imagine in their minds what they will become in the future. . . . Thus man who looks to the Way does not try to track down what has disappeared, does not try to trace the source of what springs up. This is the point at which debate comes to a stop. [292]

c. Limitation in Space and Time ⇌ Nonlimitation in Space and Time = Relative Knowledge ⇌ Absolute Knowledge

As knowledge of form and of limitation in space and time, perceptual knowledge (knowledge of parts) is relative knowledge of size and duration of things:

Compare the area within the four seas with all that is between heaven and earth — is it not like one little anthill in a vast marsh? Compare the Middle Kingdom with the area within the four seas — is it not like one tiny grain in a great storehouse? [176] Calculate the time [man] is alive and it cannot compare to the time before he was born. [177]

Conversely, as knowledge of formlessness and of nonlimitation in space and time, conceptual knowledge (knowledge of the whole) is nonrelative or absolute knowledge of things. Consequently, the relation between perceptual knowledge (knowledge of parts) and conceptual knowledge (knowledge of the whole) that forms simple apprehension (perfection of knowledge) can be expressed by the formula:

Simple Apprehension (Perfection of Knowledge) = Perceptual Knowledge (Knowledge of Parts) ⇌ Conceptual Knowledge (Knowledge of the Whole) = Form ⇌ Formlessness (First Cycle of the Way and of Simple Apprehension) = Limitation in Space and Time ⇌ Nonlimitation in Space and Time (Second Cycle of the Way and of Simple Apprehension) = Relative Knowledge ⇌ Absolute Knowledge.

Thus, perfection of knowledge demands that absolute knowledge complement the relative knowledge of the size and duration of things:

> Therefore great wisdom observes both far and near, and for that reason recognizes small without considering it paltry, recognizes large without considering it unwieldy, for it knows that there is no end to the weighing of things [i.e. to relative knowledge]. It has a clear understanding of past and present [i.e. of the relative knowledge of duration], and for that reason it spends a long time without finding it tedious, a short time without fretting at its shortness, for it knows that time has no stop. It perceives the nature of fullness and emptiness [i.e. of relative knowledge], and for that reason it does not delight if it acquires something nor worry if it loses it, for it knows that there is no constancy to the division of lots [i.e. to relativity]. [177]

More will be said about perceptual knowledge (knowledge of parts), as relative knowledge of quantity and quality, in the sections dealing with the conversions of the sixth and seventh cycles of the Way and of simple apprehension.

d. Being ⇌ Nonbeing = Concrete Knowledge ⇌ Abstract Knowledge

Since form defines and encompasses all existing things, form represents the being of things. Consequently, as knowledge of form, perceptual knowledge (knowledge of parts) is concrete knowledge. Conversely, as knowledge of formlessness, conceptual knowledge (knowledge of the whole) is also knowledge of nonbeing, and as such it is nonconcrete or abstract knowledge. Hence, the relation between perceptual knowledge (knowledge of parts) and conceptual knowledge (knowledge of the whole) that forms simple apprehension (perfection of knowledge) can be expressed by the formula:

Simple Apprehension (Perfection of Knowledge) = Perceptual Knowledge (Knowledge of Parts) ⇌ Conceptual Knowledge (Knowledge of the Whole) = Form ⇌ Formlessness (First Cycle of the Way and of Simple Apprehension) = Being ⇌ Nonbeing (Third Cycle of the Way and of Simple Apprehension) = Concrete Knowledge ⇌ Abstract Knowledge.

According to the *Chuang Tzu*, the pursuit of the perfection of knowledge demands that abstract knowledge assist concrete knowledge:

> To use a [concrete] attribute to show that attributes are not attributes is not as good as using a nonattribute [i.e. an abstract notion] to show that attributes are not attributes. To use a horse [concrete knowledge] to show that a horse is not a horse is not as good as using a non-horse [i.e. abstract notion] to show that a horse is not a horse . . . [40]

e. Life ⇌ Death = Liveliness (fullness, motivity, turbidity, noise, and action) ⇌ Tranquility (emptiness, stillness, limpidity, silence, and inaction) = Knowledge of Change ⇌ Knowledge of Changelessness

Knowledge of the form of living things is knowledge of the change of form of the things that takes place in the course of their life:

> . . . things have their life and death — you cannot rely upon their fulfillment. One moment empty, the next moment full — you cannot depend upon their form. The years cannot be held off; time cannot be stopped. . . . The life of things is a gallop, a headlong dash — with every movement they alter, with every moment they shift. [182]

Consequently, as knowledge of form, perceptual knowledge (knowledge of parts) is also knowledge of life and knowledge of change. Conversely, as knowledge of formlessness, conceptual knowledge (knowledge of the whole) is also knowledge of death and knowledge of changelessness:

112

All that have faces, forms, voices, colors — these are all mere things . . . But things have their creation in what has no form, and their conclusion in what has no change. [198]

Accordingly, the relation between perceptual knowledge (knowledge of parts) and conceptual knowledge (knowledge of the whole) that forms simple apprehension (perfection of knowledge) can be expressed by the formula:

Simple Apprehension (Perfection of Knowledge) = Perceptual Knowledge (Knowledge of Parts) ⇌ Conceptual Knowledge (Knowledge of the Whole) = Form ⇌ Formlessness (First Cycle of the Way and of Simple Apprehension) = Life ⇌ Death (Fourth Cycle of the Way and of Simple Apprehension) = Liveliness (fullness, motivity, turbidity, noise, and action) ⇌ Tranquility (emptiness, stillness, limpidity, silence, and inaction) (Fifth Cycle of the Way and of Simple Apprehension) = Knowledge of Change ⇌ Knowledge of Changelessness.

From what has just been said above, it is not surprising that relative and concrete, perceptual knowledge is knowledge of change, and that absolute and abstract, conceptual knowledge is knowledge of changelessness.

f. Limitation in Space and Time ⇌ Nonlimitation in Space and Time = Life ⇌ Death = Liveliness (fullness, motivity, turbidity, noise, and action) ⇌ Tranquility (emptiness, stillness, limpidity, silence, and inaction) = Knowledge of Mortality ⇌ Knowledge of Immortality

Life is a process that is limited by its location and by its duration. As such, life is a limitation in space and time. But knowledge of life, as limitation in space and time, is knowledge of mortality. Consequently, the perceptual knowledge of life, as limitation in space and time, is knowledge of mortality. Conversely, the conceptual knowledge of nonlimitation in space and time is also knowledge of immortality. Hence, immortality is nonlimitation in space and time. Indeed, the *Chuang Tzu* imagines immortal Perfect Man, that is to say, a man who would not be limited in time, as nonlimited in space:

> The Perfect Man is godlike [i.e. immortal, or nonlimited by time]. Though the great swamps blaze, they cannot burn him; though the great rivers freeze, they cannot chill him; though swift lightning splits the hills and howling gales shake the sea, they cannot frighten him. A man like this rides the clouds and mist, straddles the sun and moon, and wanders beyond the four seas [for he is not limited by space]. [46]

Consequently, the relation between perceptual knowledge (knowledge of parts) and conceptual knowledge (knowledge of the whole) that forms simple apprehension (perfection of knowledge) can be described by the formula:

Simple Apprehension (Perfection of Knowledge) = Perceptual Knowledge (Knowledge of Parts) $\rightleftharpoons$ Conceptual Knowledge (Knowledge of the Whole) = Form $\rightleftharpoons$ Formlessness (First Cycle of the Way and of Simple Apprehension) = Limitation in Space and Time $\rightleftharpoons$ Nonlimitation in Space and Time (Second Cycle of the Way and of Simple Apprehension) = Life $\rightleftharpoons$ Death (Fourth Cycle of the Way and of Simple Apprehension) = Liveliness (fullness, motivity, turbidity, noise, and action) $\rightleftharpoons$ Tranquility (emptiness, stillness, limpidity, silence, and inaction) (Fifth Cycle of the Way and of Simple Apprehension) = Knowledge of Mortality $\rightleftharpoons$ Knowledge of Immortality.

Since man cherishes life and fears death, he finds life acceptable and death unacceptable. But the formula of simple apprehension above equates acceptable life with mortality, which man fears and, therefore, finds unacceptable, and at the same time equates unacceptable death with immortality that man desires and, therefore, finds acceptable. Thus, acceptable life cannot be separated from the notion of unacceptable mortality, and unacceptable death cannot be separated from the notion of acceptable immortality. This means two things: First, that on the level of judgement of acceptability and unacceptability there is no distinction between acceptable life/unacceptable mortality and unacceptable death/acceptable immortality, or as the *Chuang Tzu* puts it: "Why don't you just make him see that life and death are the same story, that acceptable and unacceptable are on a single string?" [72] And, second, that the acceptability of life that is also unacceptability of mortality and the unacceptability of death that is also the acceptability of immortality are delusions of the mind:

How do I know that loving life is not a delusion? How do I know that in hating death I am not like a man who, having left home in his youth, has forgotten the way back? [47]

Consequently, since life and death are equally acceptable and unacceptable, the sage follower of the Way must equally love his life and his death:

The Great Clod burdens me with form, labors me with life, eases me in old age, and rests me in death. So if I think well of my life, for the same reason I must think well of my death. [80] [The sage] delights in early death; he delights in old age; he delights in the beginning; he delights in the end. [81]

Lastly, the formula of simple apprehension (perfection of knowledge) above shows that, in addition to being nonlimitation in space and time, immortality is also tranquility (emptiness, stillness, limpidity, silence, and inaction). Moreover, the formula above shows that death and mortality are the prerequisites to immortality, and, since death and mortality are major causes of man's unhappiness, immortality is a state of major happiness. The *Chuang Tzu* describes such a nonlimited, tranquil and happy immortality in the following anecdote:

When Chuang Tzu went to Ch'u, he saw an old skull, all dry and parched. He poked it with his carriage whip and then asked, "Sir, were you greedy for life and forgetful of reason, and so came to this? Was your state overthrown and did you bow beneath the ax, and so came to this? Did you do

115

some evil deed and were you ashamed to bring disgrace upon your parents and family, and so came to this? Was it through the pangs of cold and hunger that you came to this? Or did your springs and autumns pile up until they brought you to this?"

When he had finished speaking, he dragged the skull over and, using it for a pillow, lay down to sleep.

In the middle of the night, the skull came to him in a dream and said, "You chatter like a rhetorician and all your words betray the entanglements of a living man. The dead know nothing of these! Would you like to hear a lecture on the dead?"

"Indeed," said Chuang Tzu.

The skull said, "Among the dead there are no rulers above, no subjects below, and no chores of the four seasons. With nothing to do, our springs and autumns [i.e. time] are as endless as heaven and earth [i.e. space]. A king facing south on his throne could have no more happiness than this!"

Chuang Tzu couldn't believe this and said, "If I got the Arbiter of Fate to give you a body again, make you some bones and flesh, return you to your parents and family and your old home and friends, you would want that, wouldn't you?"

The skull frowned severely, wrinkling up its brow. "Why would I throw away more happiness than that of a king on a throne and take on the troubles of a human being again?" it said. [193—94]

The notion of happy immortality that emerges from the process of simple apprehension (perfection of knowledge) is that of personal immortality, for only a conscious individual can experience happiness. As such, it is at odds with the notion of cosmic immortality, described in Chapter One, for cosmic immortality is a depersonalized immortality. Indeed, as explained in Chapter One, the sixth and seventh cycles of the Way, namely, Multiplicity $\rightleftharpoons$ Oneness, and Diversity $\rightleftharpoons$ Sameness, account for the notion of cosmic immortality that consists of a process of destruction and pulping together of all forms of being and life for the purpose of their re-creation in novel forms of being and life. For this reason, after death, even a sage might become a willow, a rooster, a rat's liver, a bug's arm, or a pair of cartwheels. It is clear then that the *Chuang Tzu's* notion of personal immortality clashes with the *Chuang Tzu's* notion of cosmic immortality.

But is it possible to reconcile the notion of personal immortality with the notion of cosmic immortality? According to Indian thought, such a reconciliation is possible on the condition of introducing into it the notions of the soul and of metempsychosis. Indeed, in order to enjoy personal immortality, the soul must prepare and cleanse itself by migrating through the Chain of Being, from its lowliest manifestations in minerals, plants, and animals to its highest manifestation in the holy man. Once the soul achieves the highest degree of spiritual purity, it becomes free from the cycle of death and re-creation in novel forms, that is to say, free from cosmic immortality and, as such, can enter the domain of personal immortality of Nirvana (Nonbeing). Thus, Indian thought reconciles personal immortality and cosmic immortality by making the latter a precondition of the former.

As suggested by the following quotation, the *Chuang Tzu* is aware of the notion of metempsychosis that is needed for the reconciliation of personal and cosmic immortality:

> To men such as these [Meng-tzu Fan and Master Ch'in-chang], how could there be any question of putting life first or death last? They borrow the forms of different creatures and house them in the same body. [87]

Yet the *Chuang Tzu* refuses to acknowledge the need for such a reconciliation of personal and cosmic immortality:

> Now, having had the audacity to take on human form once, if I should say, 'I don't want to be anything but a man! Nothing but a man!', the Creator would surely regard me as a most inauspicious sort of person. So now I think of heaven and earth as a great furnace, and the Creator as a skilled smith. Where could he send me that would not be all right? I will go off to sleep peacefully, and then with a start I will wake up. [85]

By the same token, the *Chuang Tzu* does not deny the possibility of a reconciliation of personal immortality with cosmic immortality:

> Yi Erh-tzu said, ". . . How do you know that the Creator will not wipe away my tattoo, stick my nose back on again, and let me ride on the

process of completion and follow after you, Master?"
"Ah – we can never tell," said Hsü Yu. [89–90]

In other words, the *Chuang Tzu* leaves in abeyance the problem of such a reconciliation. Why is that so? Although the *Chuang Tzu* does not give a direct answer to this question, it is possible to entertain the following conjecture. Indeed, as just explained, such a reconciliation demands the introduction of the notion of the soul. But the notion of the soul is the spiritualized notion of the Ego/Self. Since the teachings of the *Chuang Tzu* advocates the denial of the Ego/Self, or "emptying of the mind," as a means to pain-avoidance, the notion of the soul, as spiritualized Ego/Self, would have been in flagrant contradiction with these teachings and, therefore, out of place in them. This seems to explain why the *Chuang Tzu* is loath to tackle the problem of the reconciliation of the notion of personal immortality with the notion of cosmic immortality.

g. Multiplicity ⇌ Oneness; Diversity ⇌ Sameness = Relative Knowledge ⇌ Absolute Knowledge = Knowledge of Presence ⇌ Knowledge of Essence

We have seen (See Section c. above) that, as knowledge of limitation in space and time, perceptual knowledge (knowledge of parts) is relative knowledge of size and duration. As knowledge of form, however, perceptual knowledge (knowledge of parts) is also knowledge of the multiplicity of forms and consequently is numerically relative knowledge. Thus, as relative knowledge of size, duration, and number, perceptual knowledge (knowledge of parts) is quantitative relative knowledge. By the same token, as knowledge of form, perceptual knowledge (knowledge of parts) is also knowledge of the diversity of forms and consequently is qualitative relative knowledge. In other words, perceptual knowledge (knowledge of parts) is both quantitative and qualitative relative knowledge. As such, perceptual knowledge (knowledge of parts) is knowledge of the presence of things. Conversely, as knowledge of formlessness, conceptual knowledge (knowledge of the whole) is non-quantitative, non-qualitative and absolute knowledge, that is to say, a knowledge of the non-presence, or better, a knowledge of the essence of things:

> If a thing has no form, then numbers cannot express its dimensions, and if it cannot be encompassed, then numbers cannot express its size [i.e. there cannot be any quantitative relative knowledge]. We can use words to talk about the coarseness of things and we can use our minds to visualize the fineness of things [i.e. qualitative relative knowledge]. But what words cannot describe and the mind cannot succeed in visualizing — this has nothing to do with coarseness or fineness. [178]

Thus, the relation between perceptual knowledge (knowledge of parts) and conceptual knowledge (knowledge of the whole) that forms simple apprehension (perfection of knowledge) can be described by the formula:

Simple Apprehension (Perfection of Knowledge) = Form ⇌ Formlessness (First Cycle of the Way and of Simple Apprehension) = Multiplicity ⇌ Oneness (Sixth Cycle of the Way and of Simple Apprehension) = Diversity ⇌ Sameness (Seventh Cycle of the Way and of Simple Apprehension) = Relative Knowledge ⇌ Absolute Knowledge = Knowledge of Presence ⇌ Knowledge of Essence.

h. Multiplicity ⇌ Oneness; Diversity ⇌ Sameness = Relative Knowledge ⇌ Absolute Knowledge = Subjective Knowledge ⇌ Objective Knowledge = Individual Knowledge ⇌ Universal Knowledge

As quantitative and qualitative relative knowledge, perceptual knowledge (knowledge of parts) is also subjective knowledge, because the quantity and the quality of things represent a value to the individual. Thus, as quantitative and qualitative relative knowledge, perceptual knowledge (knowledge of parts) is subjective and individual knowledge. According to the *Chuang Tzu*, there are three subjective and individual points of view that affect perceptual knowledge (knowledge of parts). First, there is the point of view of subjective differences:

> From the point of view of differences, if we regard a thing as big because there is a certain bigness to it, then among all the ten thousand things there are none that are not big. If we regard a thing as small because there is a certain smallness to it, then among the ten thousand things there are none that are not small. If we know that heaven and earth are tiny grains and the tip of a hair is a range of mountains, then we have perceived the law of difference. [179]

Second, there is the point of view of utilitarian function:

> From the point of view of function, if we regard a thing as useful because there is a certain usefulness to it, then among all the ten thousand things there are none that are not useful. If we regard a thing as useless because there is a certain uselessness to it, then among the ten thousand things there are none that are not useless. If we know that east and west are mutually opposed but that one cannot do without the other [i.e. the distinction between the useful and the useless], then we can estimate the degree of function [i.e. utility]. [179–80]

Third and last, there is the point of view of preference:

> From the point of view of preference, if we regard a thing as right because there is a certain right to it, then among the ten thousand things there are none that are not right. If we regard a thing as wrong because there is a certain wrong to it, then among the ten thousand things there are none that are not wrong. If we know that [Emperor] Yao and [the ruler] Chieh each thought himself right and condemned the other as wrong, then we may understand how there are preferences in behavior. . . . Looking at it this way, we see that struggling or giving way, behaving like a Yao or like a Chieh, may be at one time noble and at another time mean. It is impossible to establish any constant rule. [180]

120

According to the *Chuang Tzu*, subjective and individual perceptual knowledge (knowledge of parts) is a fragment of the knowledge of the whole, or universal knowledge, and, as such, cannot be true knowledge:

> Nieh Ch'üeh asked Wang Ni, "Do you know what all things agree in calling right?"
> "How would I know that?" said Wang Ni.
> "Do you know that you don't know it?"
> "How would I know that?"
> "Then do things know nothing?"
> "How would I know that? However, suppose I try saying something. What way do I have of knowing that if I say I know something I don't really not know it? Or what way do I have of knowing that if I say I don't know something I don't really in fact know it? Now let me ask *you* some questions. If a man sleeps in a damp place, his back aches and he ends up half paralyzed, but is this true of a loach? If he lives in a tree, he is terrified and shakes with fright, but is this true of a monkey? Of these three creatures, then, which one knows the proper place to live? Men eat the flesh of grass-fed and grain-fed animals, deer eat grass, centipedes find snakes tasty, and hawks and falcons relish mice. Of these four, which knows how food ought to taste? Monkeys pair with monkeys, deer go out with deer, and fish play around with fish. Men claim that Mao-ch'iang and Lady Li were beautiful, but if fish saw them they would dive to the bottom of the stream, if birds saw them they would fly away, and if deer saw them they would break into a run. Of these four, which knows how to fix the standard of beauty for the world?" [45—46]

Thus, as relative knowledge, perceptual knowledge (knowledge of parts) is also subjective and individual knowledge. Conversely, as absolute knowledge, conceptual knowledge (knowledge of the whole) is objective and universal knowledge. Since objective and universal knowledge is the antithesis of subjective and individual knowledge, the harmonious cooperation between objective and universal conceptual knowledge (knowledge of the whole) and subjective and individual perceptual knowledge (knowledge of parts) results in an unbiased, open-ended knowledge. Indeed, in the following parable, where the Lord of the River represents knowledge of parts and, therefore, perceptual knowledge, and Jo of the North

121

Sea represents knowledge of the whole and, therefore, conceptual knowledge, the *Chuang Tzu* says the following:

> "Well then," said the Lord of the River, "what should I do and what should I not do? How am I to know in the end what to accept and what to reject, what to abide by and what to discard?"
> Jo of the North Sea said, "From the point of view of the Way, what is noble or what is mean? These are merely what are called endless changes . . . What is few, or what is many? These are merely what are called boundless turnings . . . Be stern like the ruler of a state — he grants no private favor. Be benign and impartial like the god of the soil at the sacrifice — he grants no private blessing [i.e. be objective] . . . Embrace the ten thousand things universally — how could there be one you should give special support to? This is called being without bent [i.e. unbiased]. When the ten thousand things are unified and equal, then which is short and which is long?" [181–82]

Accordingly, the relation between perceptual knowledge (knowledge of parts) and conceptual knowledge (knowledge of the whole) that forms simple apprehension (perfection of knowledge) can be expressed by the formula:

Simple Apprehension (Perfection of Knowledge) = Perceptual Knowledge (Knowledge of Parts) ⇌ Conceptual Knowledge (Knowledge of the Whole) = Multiplicity ⇌ Oneness (Sixth Cycle of the Way and of Simple Apprehension) = Diversity ⇌ Sameness (Seventh Cycle of the Way and of Simple Apprehension) = Relative Knowledge ⇌ Absolute Knowledge = Subjective Knowledge ⇌ Objective Knowledge = Individual Knowledge ⇌ Universal Knowledge.

i. Multiplicity ⇌ Oneness; Diversity ⇌ Sameness = Knowledge of the Particular ⇌ Knowledge of the General

As knowledge of form and of the multiplicity and diversity of forms, perceptual knowledge (knowledge of parts) is also knowledge of the individual characteristics of each and all of these forms. In other words, perceptual knowledge (knowledge of parts) is knowledge of the particular. Conversely, as knowledge of formlessness, oneness and sameness, conceptual knowledge (knowledge of the whole) is knowledge of the non-particular, that is to say, knowledge of the general. Thus, the relation between perceptual knowledge (knowledge of parts) and conceptual knowledge (knowledge of the whole) that forms simple apprehension (perfection of knowledge) can be expressed by the formula:

Simple Apprehension (Perfection of Knowledge) = Perceptual Knowledge (Knowledge of Parts) ⇌ Conceptual Knowledge (Knowledge of the Whole) = Form ⇌ Formlessness (First Cycle of the Way and of Simple Apprehension) = Multiplicity ⇌ Oneness (Sixth Cycle of the Way and of Simple Apprehension) = Diversity ⇌ Sameness (Seventh Cycle of the Way and of Simple Apprehension) = Knowledge of the Particular ⇌ Knowledge of the General.

As the *Chuang Tzu* puts it:

Differences are combined into sameness; sameness are broken up into differences. Now we may point to each of the hundred parts of a horse's body [and thus express knowledge of the particular] and never come up with a 'horse' [i.e. with the knowledge of the general] — yet here is the horse, tethered right before our eyes. So we take the hundred parts and set up the term 'horse.' Thus it is that hills and mountains pile up one little layer on another to reach loftiness; the Yangtze and the Yellow River combine stream after stream to achieve magnitude; and the Great Man combines and brings together things to attain generality. [290]

j. Name ⇌ Namelessness = Spoken Knowledge ⇌ Unspoken Knowledge

The perceptual knowledge of the multiplicity and diversity of forms is also knowledge of the names and words that describe the

123

things; as such, perceptual knowledge is spoken knowledge. Conversely, the conceptual knowledge of the oneness and sameness of things is a nameless and wordless knowledge, that is to say, unspoken knowledge. Consequently, the pursuit of the Way, as pursuit of simple apprehension (perfection of knowledge), demands the harmonization of the "human," spoken, perceptual knowledge (knowledge of parts) and of the "Heavenly," unspoken, conceptual knowledge (knowledge of the whole):

> To know and to speak — this gets you to the human part [i.e. to perceptual knowledge]. To know and not to speak — this gets you to the Heavenly part [i.e. to conceptual knowledge]. [355] If you talk in a worthy manner, you can talk all day long and all of it will pertain to the Way. But if you talk in an unworthy manner, you can talk all day long and all of it will pertain to mere things [i.e to perceptual knowledge only]. The perfection of the Way and things — neither words nor silence are worthy of expressing it. Not to talk, not to be silent — this is the highest form of debate. [293]

Thus, the relation between perceptual knowledge (knowledge of parts) and conceptual knowledge (knowledge of the whole) that forms simple apprehension (perfection of knowledge) can be expressed by the formula:

Simple Apprehension (Perfection of Knowledge) = Perceptual Knowledge (Knowledge of Parts) ⇌ Conceptual Knowledge (Knowledge of the Whole) = Name ⇌ Namelessness (Eighth Cycle of the Way and of Simple Apprehension) = Spoken Knowledge ⇌ Unspoken Knowledge.

k. Name ⇌ Namelessness = Language as Sounds ⇌ Language as Meaning

Perceptual knowledge of the spoken language is knowledge of the sounds of the names and words that express it. Conceptual knowledge of the spoken language is knowledge of the meaning that these names and words contain. Consequently, as cycle of perceptual knowledge (knowledge of parts) and of conceptual knowledge (knowledge ot the whole), simple apprehension (perfection of knowledge) is a cyclical transition from names and words as sounds to names and words as meaning:

> The fish trap exists because of the fish; once you've gotten the fish, you can forget the trap. The rabbit snare exists because of the rabbit; once you've gotten the rabbit, you can forget the snare. Words exist because of meaning; once you've gotten the meaning, you can forget the words. Where can I find a man who has forgotten words [as sounds] so I can have a word [as meaning] with him? [302] Names should stop when they have expressed reality . . . This is what it means to have command of reason . . . [195]

According to the *Chuang Tzu*, the "sounded" names and words represent the spoken, perceptual knowledge, whereas the meaning that these names and words convey represent the unspoken, conceptual knowledge:

> What you can look at and see are forms and colors; what you can listen to and hear are names and sounds. What a pity! – that the men of the world should suppose that form and color, name and sound [i.e. perceptual knowledge] are sufficient to convey the truth of a thing. It is because in the end they are not sufficient to convey truth that "those who know do not speak, those who speak do not know." [152]

Consequently, on the plane of language, the relation between perceptual knowledge (knowledge of parts) and conceptual knowledge (knowledge of the whole) that forms simple apprehension (perfection of knowledge) can be expressed by the formula:

Simple Apprehension (Perfection of Knowledge) = Perceptual Knowledge (Knowledge of Parts) ⇌ Conceptual Knowledge (Knowledge of the Whole) = Name ⇌ Namelessness (Eighth Cycle of the Way and of Simple Apprehension) = Spoken Knowledge ⇌ Unspoken Knowledge = Language as Sounds ⇌ Language as Meaning.

l. Table of Conversion of the Eight Cycles of the Way and of Simple Apprehension into the Twelve Cycles of Conscious Knowledge

As demonstrated above, the *Chuang Tzu* converts the eight cycles of the Way and of simple apprehension into twelve cycles that describe and define the dynamics of the conscious knowledge of simple apprehension. Twelve cycles and not thirteen, because both the conversion of the second cycle of the Way and the conversion of the sixth and seventh cycles of the Way produce the same result, namely, a cycle of relative and absolute knowledge. It is convenient and useful to represent these conversions in the following table.

When read down, this table yields some interesting observations that may help to bring into focus the *Chuang Tzu's* epistemology. Indeed, according to this table, imagination is nonfinite, or infinite, knowledge; abstract knowledge is absolute knowledge; knowledge of change is knowledge of mortality, and knowledge of changelessness is knowledge of immortality – an observation that can explain the conservatism of the conscious mind; knowledge of essence is absolute knowledge; objective knowledge is universal knowledge and knowledge of the general; and lastly, knowledge of meaning is an unspoken knowledge that cannot be put into words. Moreover, since it is the spoken knowledge of the particular, perceptual knowledge (knowledge of parts) is knowledge of definitions, and, since it is the unspoken knowledge of the general, conceptual knowledge (knowledge of the whole) is knowledge of ideas. Thus, simple apprehension is not only a cycle of transformation and cooperation of analytical knowledge and of synthetical knowledge, but also a cycle of transformation and cooperation of definitions and ideas.

Table of Conversion of the Eight Cycles of the Way and of Simple Apprehension into the Twelve Cycles of Conscious Knowledge

Eight Cycles of the Way	Twelve Cycles of Conscious Knowledge
1. Form ⇌ Formlessness	1. Formal Knowledge ⇌ Imagination
2. Limitation in Space and Time ⇌ Non-limitation in Space and Time	2. Finite Knowledge ⇌ Infinite Knowledge 3. Relative Knowledge ⇌ Absolute Knowledge
3. Being ⇌ Nonbeing	4. Concrete Knowledge ⇌ Abstract Knowledge
4. Life ⇌ Death 5. Liveliness (fullness, motivity, turbidity, noise, and action) ⇌ Tranquility (emptiness, stillness, limpidity, silence, and inaction)	5. Knowledge of Change ⇌ Knowledge of Changelessness 6. Knowledge of Mortality ⇌ Knowledge of Immortality
6. Multiplicity ⇌ Oneness 7. Diversity ⇌ Sameness	3. Relative Knowledge ⇌ Absolute Knowledge 7. Knowledge of Presence ⇌ Knowledge of Essence 8. Subjective Knowledge ⇌ Objective Knowledge 9. Individual Knowledge ⇌ Universal Knowledge 10. Knowledge of the Particular ⇌ Knowledge of the General
8. Name ⇌ Namelessness	11. Spoken Knowledge ⇌ Unspoken Knowledge 12. Language as Sounds ⇌ Language as Meaning

127

Undoubtedly, by establishing all the possible associations between the terms of the twelve cycles of conscious knowledge of the table above, one could yet discover new dimensions to the *Chuang Tzu's* epistemology. Nonetheless, this should not be done recklessly because, in the last analysis, it is impossible to determine from the text of the *Chuang Tzu* whether or not its author(s) were aware of the epistemological potential of these twelve cycles of conscious knowledge.

3. The Subconscious Knowledge or Intuition

Simple apprehension is a cycle of transformation of perceptual knowledge (knowledge of parts) and conceptual knowledge (knowledge of the whole) into one another. As such, simple apprehension is conscious knowledge. Consequently, any and all failure of simple apprehension is a failure of conscious knowlege that results in mental pain. According to the *Chuang Tzu*, the failure of conscious, simple apprehension and its resultant mental pain have two causes: First, the frustration of man's consciousness by the limitations of man's life and experiences:

> Your life has a limit but knowledge has none. If you use what is limited to pursue what has no limit, you will be in danger. If you understand this and still strive for knowledge, you will be in danger for certain! [50] Alas, the men of this world are no more than travelers, stopping now at this inn, now at that, all of them run by 'things.' They know the things they happen to encounter, but not those that they have never encountered. They know how to do the things they can do, but they can't do the things they don't know how to do. Not to know, not to be able to do — from these mankind can never escape. And yet there are those who struggle to escape from the inescapable — can you help but pity them? . . . To be limited to understanding only what is understood — this is shallow indeed! [247]

And, second, mental fatigue that results from too much thinking:

> . . . the pursuit of thought may be a danger to the mind. All the faculties that are stored up in man are a potential source of danger, and if this danger becomes real and is not averted, misfortunes will go on piling up in increasing number. [278]

Thus, on the plane of knowledge, mental pain is the result of frustration of knowledge and of mental fatigue. Accordingly, the *Chuang Tzu* says that, in order to avoid such a mental pain, man must stop thinking: "Withdraw into thoughtlessness and in this way give life to your mind." [254—55] Such a state of thoughtlessness must be the result of the denial of Reality consciousness and of Self-consciousness, that is to say, of the "emptying of the

129

mind." In turn, such an "emptying of the mind" allows the subconscious mind or "spirit" to take over the functions of the conscious mind and protect man from harm and pain:

When the eye does not see, the ear does not hear, and the mind does not not know, then your spirit will protect the body, and the body will enjoy long life. Be cautious of what is within you [i.e. of conceptual knowledge]; block off what is outside you [i.e. block off perceptual knowledge], for much knowledge will do you harm. [119]

According to the *Chuang Tzu*, the subconscious mind or "spirit" possesses a higher degree of knowledge than the conscious mind:

If you use a lack of proof to establish proofs, your proofs will be proofless. The bright-eyed man [i.e. the man who uses his conscious mind] is no more than the servant of things [of which he is conscious], but the man of spirit [i.e. the man who uses his subconscious mind] knows how to find real proofs. The bright-eyed is no match for the man of spirit — from long ago this has been the case. [361]

More precisely, the subconscious mind or "spirit" reveals itself in intuition. Intuition is a sudden flash or illumination of knowledge that occurs spontaneously without any immediately preceding, registered thought-process. For this reason, the *Chuang Tzu* calls intuition "understanding that does not understand." Since, as explained above, thought-process accounts for the mental fatigue and the mental pain of conscious knowledge, such a thoughtless intuition ("understanding that does not understand") is painless and, therefore, superior to painful, conscious knowledge:

Not to understand is to understand? To understand is not to understand? Who understands the understanding that does not understand? [243] Men all pay homage to what understanding understands, but no one understands enough to rely upon what understanding does not understand and thereby come to understand. [288] Understanding that rests in what it cannot understand is the finest. [254]

130

According to the *Chuang Tzu*, conscious knowledge or understanding is "outer knowledge" and intuition or "understanding that does not understand" is "inner knowledge":

> Not to understand [i.e. intuition] is profound; to understand [i.e. conscious knowledge] is shallow. Not to understand is to be on the inside; to understand is to be on the outside. [243]

But, as explained above, "inner knowledge" is "Heavenly," or conceptual knowledge. It is, therefore, possible to believe that the *Chuang Tzu* views intuition as a subconscious, conceptual knowledge. If this is so, the conscious, conceptual knowledge is a prerequisite for the formation of intuition. Be that as it may, the *Chuang Tzu* claims that perfection of knowledge is the result of a cooperation between conscious knowledge and intuition ("understanding that does not understand"): "Therefore, when . . . words [i.e. conscious, verbalized knowledge] come to rest at the place where understanding no longer understands [i.e. intuition], we have perfection." [272]

From what has been said before, it is clear that the *Chuang Tzu* speaks of two kinds of perfection of knowledge: (1) of the perfection of knowledge that is the result of the harmonious cooperation between perceptual knowledge (knowledge of parts) and conceptual knowledge (knowledge of the whole), and (2) of the perfection of knowledge that results from the harmonious cooperation between conscious knowledge and subconscious intuition. Since intuition is superior to conscious knowledge, the second perfection of knowledge is perforce superior to the first one.

4. Instinctual Great Wisdom or Great Knowledge

Since man's life and experience are limited in space, time, and opportunity, man's conscious knowledge and man's subconscious knowledge or "spirit" are also limited. This means that there are times and circumstances when man's conscious knowledge and man's subconscious knowledge or "spirit" cannot protect him from physical harm and mental pain. In this case, according to the *Chuang Tzu*, man must deny both conscious knowledge and subconscious knowledge or "spirit" and, in so doing, effect their replacement by Great Wisdom or Great Knowledge that is limited by nothing (cf. the substitution of self-determination by Fate):

> So it is that [conscious] knowledge has its limitations, and spirituality [i.e. the subconscious mind] has that which it can do nothing about. Even the most perfect wisdom [i.e. harmonization of conscious knowledge with subconscious intuition] can be outwitted by ten thousand schemers. Fish do not [know enough to] fear a net, but only to fear pelicans. Discard little wisdom and great wisdom will become clear. [299] Why not join with me in inaction, in tranquil quietude, in hushed purity, in harmony and leisure? Already my will is vacant and blank. I go nowhere and don't know how far I've gotten. I go and come and don't know where to stop. I've already been there and back, and I don't know when the journey is done. I ramble and relax in unbordered vastness; Great Knowledge enters in, and I don't know where it will ever end. [241]

According to the *Chuang Tzu*, the Great Wisdom or Great Knowledge that replaces the ineffectual and denied conscious and subconscious mind is "pure spirit," which is the Way of Heaven, as the Natural law of the universe. Indeed, Diagram IV in Chapter One demonstrates that denial of man's consciousness, through denial of the Self and of Reality, is responsible for the substitution of man's consciousness by the Way of Heaven and Earth. But denial of knowledge is denial of knowledge of the Self, of Reality and, therefore, of the notion "earth." Accordingly, denial of knowledge effects the substitution of man's knowledge by the Way of Heaven, as the Natural Law of the universe, and not by the Way of Heaven and Earth:

132

Pure spirit reaches in the four directions, flows now this way, now that — there is no place it does not extend to . . . It transforms and nurses the ten thousand things [for it is the Natural Law of the universe], but no one can make out its form. Its name is called One-with-Heaven. The way to purity and whiteness is to guard the [pure] spirit, this alone; guard it and never lose it, and you will become one with [pure] spirit, one with its pure essence, which communicates and mingles with the Heavenly Order [i.e. the Natural Law of the universe]. [169–70]

As a substitution of conscious and subconscious knowledge by the Way of Heaven, as the Natural Law of the universe, or "pure spirit," Great Wisdom or Great Knowledge is two things: First, it is an "outer" instinctual knowledge that protects man from the physical harm and the mental pain that result from his confrontation with his "outer" world:

Call in your knowledge [i.e. deny knowledge], unify your bearing, and the spirits will come to dwell with you. Virtue will be your beauty, the Way will be your home, and, stupid as a newborn calf, you will not try to find out the reason why. [237] Because a creature that is without knowledge does not face the perils that come from trying to set oneself up, the entanglements that come from relying upon knowledge . . . Let me become like those creatures without knowledge, that is enough. [370–371] [Be like the beasts] and joy, anger, grief, and happiness [i.e. all the painful emotions] can never enter your breast. [226]

And, second, Great Wisdom or Great Knowledge is an "inner" knowledge of the essence of the things of Creation, that is to say, an absolute knowledge of these things that is not limited by space and time, or again, the Knowledge of the Truth of Creation:

He sees in the darkest dark, hears where there is no sound. In the midst of darkness [i.e. of denied knowledge], he alone sees the dawn; in the midst of the soundless, he alone hears harmony. Therefore, in depth piled upon depth he can spy out the thing; in spirituality piled upon spirituality he can discover the essence. So in his dealings with the ten thousand things he supplies all their wants out of total nothingness [i.e. total denial of knowledge]. Racing with the hour, he seeks lodging for a night, in the great, the small, the long, the short, the near, the far. [128] When a man has the Truth [i.e. the Way of Heaven, as the Natural Law of the universe, or "pure spirit"] within himself, his spirit may move among external things. That is why the Truth is to be prized! [349]

Since it is the Way of Heaven, as the Natural Law of the universe, and, since it is neither conscious knowledge nor subconscious knowledge, it is possible to say that Great Wisdom of Great Knowledge is unconscious or instinctual knowledge. And, in doing so, one should never lose sight of the fact that, according to the *Chuang Tzu*, this unconscious or instinctual Great Wisdom or Great Knowledge is superior to both the conscious and subconscious mind.

5. Conscious Knowledge and the Fall of Mankind

This chapter has demonstrated that, according to the *Chuang Tzu*, there exist three kinds of knowledge. The first and lowest of these three kinds of knowledge is conscious knowledge that reaches perfection by means of a harmonious cooperation of perceptual knowledge (knowledge of parts) and of conceptual knowledge (knowledge of the whole). The second kind of knowledge is the subconscious knowledge or "spirit" that manifests itself in intuition. For this reason, on this second level of knowledge, perfection is the result of a harmonious cooperation between conscious knowledge and subconscious intuition. The third and highest kind of knowledge is Great Wisdom or Great Knowledge that expresses the Way of Heaven, as the Natural Law of the universe, or "pure spirit." Since of these three kinds of knowledge Great Wisdom or Great Knowledge is the highest form of knowledge and conscious knowledge is the lowest, the fact that mankind chiefly uses conscious knowledge indicates that mankind has fallen from the state of Nature. Indeed, the *Chuang Tzu* believes that once upon a time such a state of Nature did exist; it was the Age of Perfect Virtue, during which mankind possessed Great Wisdom or Great Knowledge. Since Great Wisdom or Great Knowledge is also the Way of Heaven, as the Natural Law of the universe, mankind lived in a state of Nature. And again, since Heaven represents the notion of the greater whole, such a mankind experienced total unity with Creation and, for this reason, their inborn nature was whole. Such a mankind was satisfied with its life and, consequently, did not want to change it. Moreover, because they possessed Great Wisdom or Great Knowledge, the men of the Age of Perfect Virtue had no need for conscious knowledge. Consequently, their actions were not conscious, but spontaneous responses to their natural needs. Finally, because they were in total harmony with the Way of Heaven, the men of Age of Perfect Virtue were in a permanent state of Heavenly joy. [105, 173, 172].

Nonetheless, in spite of the bliss that it enjoyed in the state of Nature, mankind succumbed to the pride of conscious knowledge, which, according to the *Chuang Tzu*, the men of the Age of Perfect Virtue potentially possessed, but never used. As a result of the temptations of conscious knowledge, mankind fell. Since the state of Nature was a state of perfect unity with Creation, the fall of mankind shattered the unity of Creation and corrupted the inborn nature of all creatures. For this reason, the cosmos of the Age of Perfect Virtue was replaced by the chaos of subsequent times:

> This is how the great confusion [i.e. chaos] comes about, blotting out the brightness of sun and moon above, searing the vigor of hills and streams below, overturning the round of the four seasons in between. There is no insect that creeps and crawls, no creature that flutters and flies that has not lost its inborn nature. So great is the confusion of the world that comes from coveting [conscious] knowledge! [113]

By precipitating the fall of mankind from its erstwhile state of Nature and by causing the loss of its inborn nature, conscious knowledge turned men into unnatural beings. The unnaturalness of fallen mankind expressed itself in predatoriness, in the technological rape of Nature, and in the artificiality of man's life. Consequently, the artisan and the craftsman who created contraptions for plundering and changing Nature, and the so-called sage who imposed artificiality on life were the chief culprits for the fall of mankind:

> If we must use curve and plumb line, compass and square to make something right, this means cutting away its inborn nature; if we must use cords and knots, glue and lacquer to make something firm, this means violating its natural Virtue. So the crouchings and bendings of rites and music, the smiles and beaming looks of benevolence and righteousness, which are intended to comfort the hearts of the world, in fact destroy their constant naturalness. [100] That the unwrought substance [of Nature] was blighted in order to fashion implements -- this was the crime of the artisan. That the Way and its Virtue were destroyed in order to create [artificial] benevolence and righteousness — this was the fault of the sage. [106] See also [112–113, 117]

Conversely, if mankind could get rid of the artisan, of the craftsman, of the sage and, for that matter, of all the lesser champions of artificiality, such as artists and musicians, it could return to naturalness and its attendant Great Wisdom or Great Knowledge. In other words,

136

the redemption of fallen mankind and the re-creation of the Age of Perfect Virtue demanded a Cultural Revolution. [109, 110, 111]

6. Redemption of Mankind: Cultural Revolution and Utopia

By Cultural Revolution the *Chuang Tzu* means the forcible return to the Age of Perfect Virtue which was an age of pure naturalness, entirely devoid of any artificiality or unnaturalness. Such an age had existed in the hoary past before the appearance of the agents of artificiality, namely, the sage, the artisan, the craftsman and the musician. Accordingly, in order to re-create the Age of Perfect Virtue, the Cultural Revolution must eradicate the sage and proscribe the artisan, the craftsman and the musician, as well as all the artificial things and objects created by them. [110] Yet, the *Chuang Tzu* is not precise about the fate of the sage. In one passage the *Chuang Tzu* speaks of the physical elimination of the sage, as the archvillain responsible for the fall of mankind:

> Cudgel and cane the sages and let the thieves and bandits go their way; then the world will at last be well ordered! . . . And if the sage is dead and gone, then no more great thieves will arise. The world will then be peaceful and free of fuss. But until the sage is dead, great thieves will never cease to appear . . . [109]

But, in another passage, the *Chuang Tzu* seems to lean toward a prohibition of the activities of the sages:

> Put a stop to the ways of Tseng and Shih, gag the mouths of Yang and Mo, wipe out and reject benevolence and righteousness, and for the first time the Virtue of the world will reach the state of Mysterious Leveling. [111]

Be that as it may, the sage's influence must be stopped at all costs. Again, the *Chuang Tzu* is not clear as to whether the Cultural Revolution will precede or be a result of the political and social revolution that would prepare mankind for its transition toward the Age of Perfect Virtue. Indeed, mankind is to be gradually re-educated for its eventual return to the Age of Perfect Virtue. To this effect, mankind must be united into one single polity under the aegis of an emperor, or "king of the world," whose title will be Son of Heaven.

Such a title described the program of this new, all-encompassing polity. More precisely, since the purpose of this polity is to return mankind to the Age of Perfect Virtue, that is to say, to the state of Nature and to Great Wisdom or Great Knowledge, and, since Great Wisdom or Great Knowledge is the Way of Heaven, as the Natural Law of the universe, the emperor's ("king of the world's") title of Son of Heaven described the political program of the new polity. Again, since the comprehensive attribute of Heaven (see Chapter One) is inaction, the Son of Heaven will rule mankind through inaction:

> The Virtue of emperors and kings takes Heaven and earth as its ancestor, the Way and its Virtue as its master, inaction as its constant rule . . . Therefore the kings of the world in ancient times [i.e. in the Age of Perfect Virtue], though their knowledge encompassed all Heaven and earth, did not of themselves lay plans; though their power of discrimination embraced the ten thousand things, they did not of themselves expound any theories; though their abilities outshone all within the four seas, they did not of themselves act. Heaven does not give birth, yet the ten thousand things are transformed; earth does not sustain, yet the ten thousand things are nourished. The emperor and the king do not act, yet the world is benefited. [144–145]

In fact, the Son of Heaven (emperor or king of the world) would delegate action to his ministers. It would be the duty of these ministers to reform mankind for its eventual return to the state of Nature. Consequently, the Son of Heaven will choose these ministers from among those people who practiced naturalness, that is, from among those who valued the health of their body and the integrity of their inborn nature above all other things. But since the preservation of the health of one's body and of the integrity of one's inborn nature was the result of inaction, these ministers of the Son of Heaven will administer the empire through inaction:

> If the gentleman finds he has no other choice than to direct and look after the world, then the best course for him is inaction. As long as there is inaction, he may rest in the true form of his nature and fate. If he values his own body more than the management of the world, then he can be

entrusted with the world. If he is more careful of his own body than of the management of the world, then the world can be handed over to him. [116]

But, before sinking into inaction, these ministers of the Son of Heaven will have to impose on society the hierarchical principle of the Way of Heaven and earth:

Honor and lowliness, precedence and following are part of the workings of Heaven and earth, and from them the sage draws his model . . . If Heaven and earth, the loftiest in spirituality, have yet their sequence of honorable and lowly, of preceder and follower, how much more must be the way of man! In the ancestral temple, honor is determined by degree of kinship; in the court, by degree of nobility; in the village, by degree of seniority; in the administration of affairs, by degree of worth. This is the sequence of the Great Way. [146]

Such a hierarchical structuration of society would be upheld by means of rewards and punishments:

Having made clear rewards and punishments, they could be certain that stupid and wise were in their proper place, that eminent and lowly were rightly ranked, that good and worthy men as well as unworthy ones showed their true form, that all had duties suited to their abilities, that all acted in accordance with their titles. It was in this way that superiors were served, inferiors were shepherded, external things were ordered, the inner man was trained. Knowledge and scheming were unused, yet all found rest in Heaven. This was called the Great Peace, the Highest Government. [147]

According to the *Chuang Tzu*, the elimination of the agents of conscious knowledge from society, namely, the sage, the artisan, the craftsman, the artist, and the musician, and the imposition on society of the hierarchical discipline described above would cause mankind to lose its conscious knowledge and to acquire naturalness. In turn, the total loss of conscious knowledge and the acquisition of naturalness are the preconditions to mankind's attainment of Great Wisdom or Great Knowledge. When mankind possesses Great Wisdom or

140

Great Knowledge, mankind will live in an Age of Perfect Virtue. The Age of Perfect Virtue will witness the dissolution of the authority of the Son of Heaven and his ministers, as well as of the hierarchical system that the latter imposed on it in the past, for mankind too would act through inaction, that is, spontaneously and well:

> In Nan-yüeh there is a city and its name is The Land of Virtue Established. Its people are foolish and naïve, few in thoughts of self, scant in desires. They know how to make, but not how to lay away; they give, but look for nothing in return. They do not know what accords with right, they do not know what conforms to ritual. Uncouth, uncaring, they move recklessly — and this way they tread the path of the Great Method. [211] In an age of Perfect Virtue the worthy are not honored, the talented are not employed. Rulers are like the high branches of a tree, the people like the deer of the fields. They do what is right but they do not know that this is righteousness. They love one another but they do not know that this is benevolence. They are truehearted but do not know that this is loyalty. They are trustworthy but do not know that this is good faith. They wriggle around like insects, performing services for one another, but do not know that they are being kind. Therefore they move without leaving any trail behind, act without leaving any memory of their deeds. [138]

There is no doubt that the *Chuang Tzu's* Age of Perfect Virtue is quite similar to Jean-Jacques Rousseau's description of man in a state of Nature. Be that as it may, the *Chuang Tzu's* elaboration of the vision of the Age of Perfect Virtue is above all a logical extension of its quest for pain-avoidance. Since conscious knowledge, or generally speaking, consciousness is a source of mental pain, mankind must strive toward a stage where conscious knowledge would no longer exist. But to the extent that mankind needs conscious knowledge for survival and pain-avoidance, the absence of conscious knowledge must be filled by an unconscious knowledge of the world, that is to say, by Great Wisdom or Great Knowledge of the Natural Law of the universe.

7. Conclusion

This chapter has presented the *Chuang Tzu's* recommendations on how to avoid pain that results from knowledge. In doing so, this chapter has demonstrated that, as far as the *Chuang Tzu* is concerned, there exist three levels of knowledge. First, conscious knowledge that reaches perfection when it is a harmonious cooperation of the human, perceptual knowledge (knowledge of parts) and of the Heavenly, conceptual knowledge (knowledge of the whole). Second, a knowledge that is a combination of conscious knowledge and of subconscious knowledge or intuition ("spirit") that achieves perfection when conscious knowledge and subconscious knowledge or intuition ("spirit") are in perfect harmony. According to the *Chuang Tzu*, subconscious knowledge or intuition ("spirit") is, in fact, subconscious, conceptual knowledge. Third and last, the highest and ultimate knowledge, Great Wisdom or Great Knowledge, is a knowledge that man can possess as soon as he can divest himself of both conscious knowledge and subconscious knowledge or intuition ("spirit"). Once rid of these two kinds of knowledge, man loses any sense of distinction between himself and Creation and experiences a total unity and sameness with the world. At that stage, man's knowledge is a channel of the Natural Law of the universe or "pure spirit" of Creation. Thus, Great Wisdom or Great Knowledge is knowledge of the Natural Law of the universe and, as such, is supreme knowledge. Incidentally, one finds a similar gradation of knowledge in Indian thought, where total unity and sameness with the world appears as the state of *kevala*, and where the resultant knowledge is an Absolute Consciousness, for it includes simultaneously all Creation in its undivided totality. Among the Western mystics, total unity and sameness with the world appears as the state of "mystical unity," and the resultant knowledge, as knowledge of God.

The *Chuang Tzu's* teachings on knowledge present a problem. Indeed, the *Chuang Tzu's* heaviest stress is on the perfection of conscious knowledge. Yet, avowedly, the harmonious combination of conscious knowledge and of subconscious knowledge or intuition ("spirit") is a higher stage of knowledge, and Great Wisdom or Great Knowledge is the highest stage of knowledge. Why, then, does the

142

Chuang Tzu stress so heavily the seemingly least important, conscious knowledge? One can give two answers to this question: one — practical, and the other — structural. First, the practical answer: the *Chuang Tzu* overemphasizes the importance of conscious knowledge, because its main concern is ordinary pain-avoidance, which, for the most part, demands the exercise of conscious knowledge. And, second, the structural answer: the *Chuang Tzu* overemphasizes the importance of conscious knowledge, because without the latter there cannot be any higher stages of knowledge. Indeed, without conscious knowledge there cannot be any combination of conscious knowledge and subconscious knowledge or intuition ("spirit"), the more so, since the latter is subconscious conceptual knowledge. Similarly, without conscious knowledge there cannot be any Great Wisdom or Great Knowledge, because the latter would be the result of the denial of conscious knowledge and of subconscious knowledge or intuition ("spirit"). One can also say that since the achievement of Great Wisdom or Great Knowledge demands a Taoist Revolution and a Taoist Utopia, Great Wisdom or Great Knowledge belongs to a distant future and, as such, is not immediately relevant. Hence, the *Chuang Tzu's* marked emphasis on conscious knowledge and on the combination of conscious knowledge with subconscious knowledge or intuition ("spirit").

Chapter Four

PAIN-AVOIDANCE ON THE PLANE OF BEHAVIOR

The task of this chapter is to present and explain the *Chuang Tzu's* teachings on pain-avoidance, on the plane of behavior. Because it is plain and manifest in the text, the *Chuang Tzu's* teachings on behavioral pain-avoidance does not require any methodological approach. For this reason, this chapter may strike the readers as being anti-climactic. Yet, without this chapter, the book would be incomplete, for its central thesis is to explain the *Chuang Tzu* as a vast and complex teaching of pain-avoidance. According to the *Chuang Tzu*, since the Way of Heaven and Earth is the ultimate road to pain-avoidance and, at the same time, the Natural Law of the universe, the pain-avoiding behavior of the follower of the Way must perforce be a behavior that is faithful to Nature. As such, the behavior of the follower of the Way is the pursuit of naturalness and, by the same token, a repudiation of any kind of artificiality.

More precisely, since Nature has given him life and a body to house it, the follower of the Way must behave in such a manner as to preserve life through the preservation of his body from artificiality. In fact, the preservation and care of the life-housing body is natural art and, as such, the only art of the follower of the Way:

> Lord Yüan of Sung wanted to have some pictures painted. The crowd of court clerks all gathered in his presence, received their drawing panels, and took their places in line, licking their brushes, mixing their inks, so many of them that there were more outside the room than inside it. There was one clerk who arrived late, sauntering in without the slightest haste. When he received his drawing panel, he did not look for a place in line, but went straight to his own quarters. The ruler sent someone to see what he was doing, and it was found that he had taken off his robes, stretched out his legs, and was sitting there naked. "Very good," said the ruler. "This is a true artist!" [228]

Since life manifests itself in the body, the preservation of life is the preservation of the body. In turn, the preservation of the body means non-expenditure of its vitality through inaction, which is the comprehensive attribute of Heaven (see Chapter One). And cultivation of inaction is avoidance of the vitality-draining efforts of everyday life. Consequently, by cultivating inaction, the follower of the Way becomes one with Heaven:

> But why is abandoning the affairs of the world worth while, and why is forgetting life worth while? If you abandon the affairs of the world, your body will be without toil. If you forget life, your vitality will be unimpaired. With your body complete and your vitality made whole again, you may become one with Heaven . . . When the body and vitality are without flaw, this is called being able to shift. Vitality added to vitality, you return to become the Helper of Heaven. [197–98]

According to the *Chuang Tzu*, total inaction is beyond any man's ken, consequently, striving for inaction is only an ideal striving:

> A man of true brightness and purity who can enter into simplicity, who can return to the primitive through inaction, give body to his inborn nature, and embrace his spirit, and in this way wander through the everyday world – if you had met one like that, you would have had real cause for astonishment. [136]

Thus to strive for inaction means not to act unnecessarily, that is to say, to act only when one must act:

> Roused by something outside himself, only then does he respond; pressed, only then does he move; finding he has no choice, only then does he rise up. He discards knowledge and purpose and follows along with the reasonableness of Heaven . . . So it is said, The sage rests; with rest comes peaceful ease, with peaceful ease comes limpidity, and where there is ease and limpidity, care and worry cannot get at him, noxious airs cannot assault him. Therefore his Virtue is complete and his spirit unimpaired. [168]

Again, the preservation of the body's vitality through the pursuit of inaction implies the preservation of the body's health without the efforts of any physical exercise:

146

To pant, to puff, to hail, to sip, to spit out the old breath and draw in the new, practicing bear-hangings and birth-stretchings, longevity his only concern — such is the life favored by the scholar who practices Induction, the man who nourishes his body, who hopes to live to be as old as P'eng-tzu. But to attain . . . long life without Induction. . . . — this is the Way of Heaven and earth, the Virtue of the sage. [167–68]

But, most important, the preservation of the body's vitality through inaction demands nonparticipation in the worldly competition for wealth, fame and reputation, for such a competition ruins one's health and robs one of one's serenity (cf. Chapter Two):

This is what the world honors: wealth, eminence, long life, a good name. This is what the world finds happiness in: a life of ease, rich food, fine clothes, beautiful sights, sweet sounds. This is what it looks down on: poverty, meanness, early death, a bad name. This is what it finds bitter: a life that knows no rest, a mouth that gets no rich food, no fine clothes for the body, no beautiful sights for the eye, no sweet sounds for the ear.

People who can't get these things fret a great deal and are afraid — this is a stupid way to treat the body. People who are rich wear themselves out rushing around on business, piling up more wealth than they could ever use — this is a superficial way to treat the body. People who are eminent spend night and day scheming and wondering if they are doing right — this is a shoddy way to treat the body. Man lives his life in company with worry, and if he lives a long while, till he's dull and doddering, then he has spent that much time worrying instead of dying, a bitter lot indeed! This is a callous way to treat the body. [190]

In fact, for the *Chuang Tzu*, happiness is not in the successful attainment of wealth, fame and reputation, but in the quietude and the integrity of inaction that preserves the body's vitality:

What ordinary people do and what they find happiness in — I don't know whether such happiness is in the end really happiness or not. I look at what ordinary people find happiness in, what they all make a mad dash for, racing around as though they couldn't stop — they all say they're happy with it . . . In the end is there really happiness or isn't there?

I take inaction to be true happiness, but ordinary people think it is a bitter thing. I say: perfect happiness knows no happiness . . . Perfect happiness, keeping alive — only inaction gets you close to this! [191]

In addition to the preservation of one's body's vitality through the cultivation of inaction, one must seek to preserve the integrity of his inborn nature, which is one's natural "characteristics and limitations" [132]:

> He who holds to True Rightness does not lose the original form of his inborn nature . . . The duck's legs are short, but to stretch them out would worry him; the crane's legs are long, but to cut them down would make him sad. What is long by nature needs no cutting off; what is short by nature needs no stretching. [99–100]

According to the *Chuang Tzu*, just as in the case of the body's vitality, inborn nature can be lost through striving for wealth, fame and reputation:

> From the Three Dynasties on down, everyone in the world has altered his inborn nature because of some [external] thing. The petty man? – he will risk death for the sake of profit. The knight? – he will risk it for the sake of fame. The high official? – he will risk it for family; the sage? – he will risk it for the world. All these various men go about the business in a different way, and are tagged differently when it comes to fame and reputation; but in blighting their inborn nature and risking their lives for something they are the same. [101]

Consequently, non-striving for wealth, fame and reputation can protect the inborn nature. Moreover, man can vitiate or lose his inborn nature when his senses become artificially over-refined. Indeed, over-refinement of the senses confuses man's consciousness and intensifies man's likes and dislikes and this, in turn, produces pain-bearing emotions (cf. Chapter Two):

> There are five conditions under which the inborn nature is lost. One: when the five colors confuse the eye and cause the eyesight to be unclear. Two: when the five notes confuse the ear and cause the hearing to be unclear. Three: when the five odors stimulate the nose and produce weariness and congestion in the forehead. Four: when the five flavors dull the mouth, causing the sense of taste to be impaired and lifeless. Five: when

likes and dislikes unsettle the mind and cause the inborn nature to become volatile and flighty. These five are all a danger to life. [140–41]

As a matter of fact, it is for this reason that artisans, craftsmen, artists, and musicians will be forciby prevented from plying their sense-confusing trades in the Taoist Utopia of the future! (cf. Chapter Three). Thus, in order to protect his inborn nature from the artificially induced over-refinement of the senses, the follower of the Way will protect his senses from the temptations of all artificial stimuli:

> When men hold on to their eyesight, the world will no longer be dazzled.
> When men hold on to their hearing, the world will no longer be wearied.
> When men hold on to their wisdom, the world will no longer be confused.
> When men hold on to their Virtue, the world will no longer go awry.
> [111]

Lastly, inborn nature can be destroyed by the practice of benevolence and righteousness.. According to the *Chuang Tzu*, benevolence and righteousness exist in one's inborn nature as a monolithic whole, that is to say, as an untapped potential. For this reason, any and all attempt at practicing benevolence and righteousness and, for that matter, displaying any qualities of one's inborn nature is a violation of their natural integrity:

> There is such a thing as completion and injury – Mr. Chao playing the lute is an example. There is such a thing as no completion and no injury – Mr. Chao not playing the lute is an example. [41–42] The Great Way is not named; Great Discriminations are not spoken; Great Benevolence is not benevolent; Great Modesty is not humble; Great Daring does not attack. If the Way is made clear, it is not the Way. If discriminations are put into words, they do not suffice. If benevolence has a constant object, it cannot be universal. If modesty is fastidious, it cannot be trusted. If daring attacks, it cannot be complete. These five are all round [i.e. perfect], but they tend toward the square [i.e. imperfection]. [44]

That those who practice benevolence and righteousness destroy their inborn nature can be ascertained by the fact that, at best, they spend their time worrying about the failures of benevolence and righteousness in the world and, at worst, that they perish from the effects of their moral pride and indignation:

> Nowadays the benevolent men of the age lift up weary eyes, worrying over the ills of the world . . . Those benevolent men — how much worrying they do! [100] Everyone in the world risks his life for something. If he risks it for benevolence and righteousness, then custom names him a gentleman; if he risks it for goods and wealth, then custom names him a petty man. The risking is the same, and yet we have a gentleman here, a petty man there. In destroying their lives and blighting their inborn nature, Robber Chih and Po Yi [a historical figure who starved himself to death out of moral indignation] were two of a kind. [102] . . . Do not be a petty man — return to and obey the Heaven within you; do not be a gentleman — follow the reason of Heaven. [334]

Thus, as pursuit of naturalness, the behavior of the follower of the Way seeks the preservation of the body, of its vitality, and of its inborn nature from the dangers of exertion, nervousness or surfeit that accrue from the over-titillation of the senses, and from the temptations of wealth and fame, benevolence and righteousness. This does not mean that the follower of the Way must be either a recluse or a hermit. In fact, the follower of the Way is very much a part of his world. But he participates in it as marginally as possible, that is to say, only when he has to. Such a marginal participation can be achieved by "emptying" one's mind:

> Do not be an embodier of fame; do not be a storehouse of schemes; do not be an undertaker of projects; do not be a proprietor of wisdom. Embody to the fullest what has no end and wander where there is no trail [i.e., follow the Way of Heaven and Earth]. Hold on to all that you have received from Heaven but do not think you have gotten anything. Be empty, that is all. [97]

This marginal participation also means formal respect of morality (benevolence and righteousness), coupled with moral non-involvement and simplicity of behavior:

> The Perfect Man of ancient times used benevolence as a path to be borrowed, righteousness as a lodge to take shelter in. He wandered in the free and easy wastes, ate in the plain and simple fields, and strolled in the garden of no bestowal. Free and easy, he rested in inaction; plain and simple, it was not hard for him to live; bestowing nothing, he did not have to hand things out. [162]

Free from involvement and restraint, as well as from effort, the follower of the Way can grasp the world as an undivided whole, or Oneness (Sixth Cycle of the Way):

> I am going to try speaking some reckless words and I want you to listen to them recklessly. How will that be? The sage leans on the sun and moon, tucks the universe under his arm, merges himself with things, leaves the confusion and muddle as it is, and looks on slaves as exalted. Ordinary men strain and struggle; the sage is stupid and blockish. He takes part in ten thousand ages and achieves simplicity in oneness. For him, all the ten thousand things are what they are, and thus they enfold each other. [47]

His unified vision of the world affords him a clear and objective perception of all things: ". . . if you were to hide the world in the world, so that nothing could get away, this would be the final reality of the constancy of things." [81]

For the *Chuang Tzu* freedom from any effort, restraint or involvement does not imply freedom from responsibility to the family. Indeed, time and again, directly or indirectly, the *Chuang Tzu* stresses the fact that both the family into which one is born and the family that one creates are gifts from Heaven and, as such, must be cherished and protected.

Freedom from any effort, restraint or involvement, or again, from any participation in mankind's strivings develops a tranquil mind, that is to say, a mind that is empty, still, limpid, silent, and inactive. But emptiness, stillness, limpidity, silence, and inaction represent the fifth attribute of Heaven (see Chapter One, the Fifth Cycle of the Way). No wonder, then, that such a tranquil mind is a superior and exultant mind that can effortlessly manage men and circumstances:

Emptiness, stillness, limpidity, silence, inaction — these are the level of Heaven and earth, the substance of the Way and its Virtue. Therefore the emperor, the king, the sage rest in them. Resting, they may be empty; empty, they may be full; and fullness is completion. Empty, they may be still; still, they may move; moving, they may acquire. Still, they may rest in inaction; resting in inaction, they may demand success from those who are charged with activities. Resting in inaction, they may be merry; being merry, they may shun the place of care and anxiety, and the years of their life will be long. [142–43]

Again, an empty, still, limpid, and inactive mind is a mind that preserves its natural simplicity from any and all artifice. In turn, a mind that has preserved its natural simplicity is a perfectly beautiful mind:

In stillness you will be a sage, in action a king. Resting in inaction, you will be honored; of unwrought simplicity, your beauty will be such that no one in the world may vie with you. [143] Lao Tan said, ". . . He who attains Perfect Beauty and wanders in Perfect Happiness may be called the Perfect Man." [225]

Lastly, a mind that preserves its natural simplicity is a sincere and unscheming mind and an aristocratic mind, too. Indeed, the freedom from entanglement with the sordid strivings of the hoi polloi, unswerving loyalty to one's family, detachment, a mind that is simple, superior, happy and beautiful, sincere and unscheming — these are the *Chuang Tzu's* aristocratic qualities. They dovetail with the *Chuang Tzu's* obsessive revulsion, as well as pitying contempt, toward the petty man and the middle-class gentleman. In fact, as will be illustrated presently, the pain-avoiding behavior of the follower of the Way consists either of avoiding any contacts with these contemptible petty men and gentlemen or of not acting as they do. Yet the awareness of the *Chuang Tzu's* high-mindedness on the plane of behavior must not obfuscate the fact that the follower of the Way

152

must use his empty, still, limpid, and inactive, that is to say, tranquil mind primarily for the purpose of pain-avoidance.

The aristocratic freedom and detachment from the hustle and bustle of everyday life and aloofness from vulgar people is a dangerous attitude, for it elicits resentments and harmful consequences. For this reason, the follower of the Way will strive to be modest and humble:

> . . . Then let me try telling you about a way to keep from dying. In the eastern sea there is a bird and its name is Listless. It flutters and flounces but seems to be quite helpless. It must be boosted and pulled before it can get into the air, pushed and shoved before it can get back to its nest. It never dares to be the first to advance, never dares to be the last to retreat. At feeding time, it never ventures to take the first bite, but picks only at the leftovers. So, when it flies in file, it never gets pushed aside, nor do other creatures such as men ever do it any harm. In this way it escapes disaster. [213]

In turn, modesty and humility means total absence of conceit, whether willed or unwilled:

> The straight-trunked tree is the first to be felled; the well of sweet water is the first to run dry. And you, now – you show off your wisdom in order to astound the ignorant, work at your good conduct in order to distinguish yourself from the disreputable, going around bright and shining as though you were carrying the sun and moon in your hand! That's why you can't escape! [213–14] Beauty, a fine beard, a tall stature, brawn, strength, style, bravery, decisiveness – when a man has all these to a degree that surpasses others, they will bring him trouble . . . Wisdom and knowledge, and the outward recognition they involve; bravery and decisiveness, and the numerous resentments they arouse; benevolence and righteousness, and all the responsibilities they involve – these six are what will bring you punishment. [359–60]

Again, modesty and humility means that the follower of the Way must not be overbearing, for overbearance creates resentment, and flaws one's inborn nature with the "four evils" of avidity, avarice, obstinacy, and bigotry:

153

... to be fond of plunging into great undertakings, altering and departing from the old accepted ways, hoping thereby to enhance your merit and fame – this is called avidity. To insist that you know it all, that everything be done your way, snatching from others and appropriating for your own use – this is called avarice. To see your errors but refuse to change, to listen to remonstrance but go on behaving worse than before – this is called obstinacy. When men agree with you, to commend them; when they disagree with you, to refuse to see any goodness in them even when it is there – this is called bigotry. These are the four evils. [347–48]

But not to be overbearing does not mean that the follower of the Way must seek to ingratiate himself with others, for ingratiation produces dangerous intrigues and ruins one's inborn nature by means of "eight faults," – namely: officiousness, obsequiousness, sycophancy, flattery, calumny, maliciousness, wickedness, and treachery:

To do what it is not your business to do is called officiousness. To rush forward when no one has nodded in your direction is called obsequiousness. To echo a man's opinions and try to draw him out in speech is called sycophancy. To speak without regard for what is right or wrong is called flattery. To delight in talking about other men's failings is called calumny. To break up friendships and set kinfolk at odds is called maliciousness. To praise falsely and hypocritically so as to cause injury and evil to others is called wickedness. Without thought for right and wrong, to try to face in two directions at once so as to steal a glimpse of the other party's wishes is called treachery. These eight faults inflict chaos on others and injury on the possessor. [347]

According to the *Chuang Tzu*, participation in the government and high administration of a state is without doubt the most dangerous occupation. In many places, but above all in one of its longest chapters, Chapter Twenty-Eight ["Giving Away a Throne," pp. 309–322], the *Chuang Tzu* gives a lengthy account of all the famous Chinese who served well their rulers and who died a violent and ignominious death. And, switching from the tragic to the facetious, the *Chuang Tzu* cites many amusing anecdotes about the manner in which several Taoist sages managed to avoid serving the state. Here is one example:

154

Once, when Chuang Tzu was fishing in the P'u River, the king of Ch'u sent two officials to go and announce to him: "I would like to trouble you with the administration of my realm."

Chuang Tzu held on to the fishing pole and, without turning his head, said, "I have heard that there is a sacred tortoise in Ch'u that has been dead for three thousand years. The king keeps it wrapped in cloth and boxed, and stores it in the ancestral temple. Now would this tortoise rather be dead and have its bones left behind and honored? Or would it rather be alive and dragging its tail in the mud?"

"It would rather be alive and dragging its tail in the mud," said the two officials.

Chuang Tzu said, "Go away! I'll drag my tail in the mud!" [187–88]

Similarly, the *Chuang Tzu* enjoins the avoidance of those who enrich themselves by flattering their rulers, for such people are base and loathsome individuals. Indeed, answering a sycophant who bragged of the fact that the king of Ch'in gave him a reward of one hundred chariots, Chuang Tzu said:

"When the king of Ch'in falls ill, he calls for his doctors. The doctor who lances a boil or drains an abscess receives one carriage in payment, but the one who licks his piles for him gets five carriages. The lower down the area to be treated, the larger the number of carriages. From the large number of carriages you've got, I take it you must have been treating his piles. Get out!" [357]

Conversely, the *Chuang Tzu* also enjoins the avoidance of the demagogues who are the sycophants of the rabble:

. . . he who agrees with everything his lord says and approves of everything his lord does is regarded by popular opinion as an unworthy minister. But in other cases men do not realize that the same principle should apply. If a man agrees with everything that popular opinion says and regards as good everything that popular opinion regards as good, he is not, as you might expect, called a sycophant and a flatterer. Are we to assume, then, that popular opinion . . . is more to be honored than one's lord? [138–39]

Thus, the pain-avoiding behavior of the follower of the Way consists of avoiding all governmental duties and all contacts with either court sycophants or demagogues.

Since the follower of the Way is not a hermit or a recluse, but someone who lives in the world of men, he cannot avoid coming in contact with all sorts of men who are potentially harmful to him. According to the *Chuang Tzu*, in order to avoid pain in this case, the follower of the Way, with his tranquil mind, must be true to himself, that is to say, sincere. For sincerity cannot be faked, lest it should arouse suspicion in the minds of others:

> He who lacks purity and sincerity cannot move others. Therefore he who forces himself to lament, though he may sound sad, will awaken no grief. He who forces himself to be angry, though he may sound fierce, will arouse no awe. And he who forces himself to be affectionate, though he may smile, will create no air of harmony. True sadness need make no sound to awaken grief; true anger need not show itself to arouse awe; true affection need not smile to create harmony. [349]

On the other hand, the vulgar petty man is insincere; he is a dissembler, who, for the sake of ingratiating himself with others, displays feelings that he does not have. For this reason, he exaggerates his performance and is soon unmasked as false:

> The friendship of a gentleman, they say, is insipid as water; that of a petty man, sweet as rich wine. But the insipidity of the gentleman leads to affection, while the sweetness of the petty man leads to revulsion. [215]

Consequently, the follower of the Way must stay away from the insincerity of petty men and, thus, avoid the painful necessity of breaking his relations with them, and incurring their resentment at being found out.

But too much sincerity on the part of the follower of the Way may be interpreted by others as intrusion or aggression and, for this reason, be strongly resented by them. Accordingly, in order to avoid the painful consequences of an inordinate display of sincerity, the follower of the Way must not give free rein to his sincerity, no matter how pure his intentions:

156

[Men, too,] if you press them too hard, are bound to answer you with ill-natured hearts, though they do not know why they do so . . . Can you afford to be careless? [61]

In fact, the follower of the Way must learn to display his sincerity at the right time and at the right place:

The horse lover will use a fine box to catch the dung and a giant clam shell to catch the stale. But if a mosquito or a fly lights on the horse and he slaps it at the wrong time, then the horse will break the bit, hurt its head, and bang its chest. The horse lover tries to think of everything, but his affection leads him into error. Can you afford to be careless? [63]

By the same token, the follower of the Way must avoid any painful confrontation with others by approaching them from the right side. To this effect, the follower of the Way must learn other people's dispositions and predilections. In doing so, the follower of the Way is able to confront even the fiercest individual without danger to himself:

Don't you know how the tiger trainer goes about it? He doesn't dare give the tiger any living thing to eat for fear it will learn the taste of fury by killing it. He doesn't dare give it any whole thing to eat for fear it will learn the taste of fury by tearing it apart. He gauges the state of the tiger's appetite and thoroughly understands its fierce disposition. Tigers are a different breed from men, and yet you can train them to be gentle with their keepers by following along with them. The men who get killed are the ones who go against them. [63] But if you hope to get a man, you must cage him with what he likes or you will never succeed. [260]

Thus, the follower of the Way must always be in control of his relations with other individuals. But such a control is impossible when in the presence of a crowd. For this reason, the follower of the Way must avoid any confrontation with a gathering of people, particularly when this gathering is for the purpose of games, competition, or drinking, because such pastimes invariably degenerate into violence and vulgarity:

When men get together to pit their strength in games of skill, they start off in a light and friendly mood, but usually end up in a dark and angry one, and if they go on too long they start resorting to various underhanded tricks. When men meet at some ceremony to drink, they start off in an orderly manner, but usually end up in disorder, and if they go on too long they start indulging in various irregular amusements. It is the same with all things. What starts out being sincere usually ends up being deceitful. What was simple in the beginning acquires monstrous proportions in the end. [60–61]

Finally, the *Chuang Tzu* addresses itself to the problem of pain-avoidance on the plane of speech. Indeed, men communicate with each other by means of speech, but, sooner or later, speech leads to verbal altercations that produce resentment, enmity and, consequently, pain and harm to those who are involved in them. The reason for this is the vain belief that one is right and the other is wrong. [39] Accordingly, the pain-avoiding follower of the Way must neither argue nor debate, for all arguments and debates are futile and dangerous attempts at proving oneself right and the other wrong:

Suppose you and I have had an argument. If you have beaten me instead of my beating you, then are you necessarily right and am I necessarily wrong? If I have beaten you instead of your beating me, then am I necessarily right and are you necessarily wrong? Is one of us right and the other wrong? Are both of us right or are both of us wrong? If you and I don't know the answer, then other people are bound to be even more in the dark. Whom shall we get to decide what is right? Shall we get someone who agrees with you to decide? But if he already agrees with you, how can he decide fairly? Shall we get someone who agrees with me? But if he already agrees with me, how can he decide? Shall we get someone who disagrees with both of us? But if he already disagrees with both of us, how can he decide? Shall we get someone who agrees with both of us? But if he already agrees with both of us, how can he decide? Obviously, then, neither you nor I nor anyone else can decide for each other. Shall we wait for still another person? [48]

Above all, the follower of the Way must avoid entering into any discussion of lofty matters with the untutored minds, for it would inevitably result in confusion, misunderstanding, and painful resentment:

> Great music is lost on the ears of the villagers, but play them "The Breaking of the Willow" or "Bright Flowers" and they grin from ear to ear. In the same way, lofty words make no impression on the minds of the mob. Superior words gain no hearing because vulgar words are in the majority. It is like the case of the two travelers tramping along in confusion and never getting where they are going. With all the confusion in the world these days, no matter how often I point the way, what good does it do? And if I know it does no good and still make myself do it, this too is a kind of confusion. So it is best to leave things alone and not force them. If I don't force things, at least I won't cause anyone any worry. [140]

Similarly, in his quest for pain-avoidance, the follower of the Way must avoid any and all discussion with those who are dogmatically narrow-minded, for the latter believe that they are the sole possessors of truth:

> You can't discuss the ocean with a well frog — he's limited by the space he lives in. You can't discuss ice with a summer insect — he's bound to a single season. You can't discuss the Way with a cramped scholar — he's shackled by his doctrines. [175–76]

Again, just as in his demeanor, so too in his speech the follower of the Way must be modest and humble. To this effect, he must not arouse the danger of his interlocutors by showing off his superiority: "Hence anger arises from no other cause than clever words and one-sided speeches." [61] In the same vein, in his speech, the follower of the Way must not distort the facts by exaggerating their meaning, for exaggerations produce misrepresentations and a dangerous resentment in those who suffer from them:

> Anything that smacks of exaggeration is irresponsible. Where there is irresponsibility, no one will trust what is said, and when that happens, the man who is transmitting the words will be in danger. Therefore the aphorism says, 'Transmit the established facts; do not transmit words of exaggeration.' If you do that, you will probably come out all right. [60]

159

According to the *Chuang Tzu*, in order to avoid being accused of "clever words," of "one-sided speeches," or of "exaggerations," the follower of the Way should resort either to the use of "imputed words" or to the use of "repeated words." By "imputed words," the *Chuang Tzu* designates a style of speech that consists of attributing the views and opinions of the speaker to a remote or fictional third party, so that any resultant counter-argument or resentment will be directed against this remote or fictional third party, and not against the speaker himself:

> These imputed words which make up nine tenths of it [i.e. the speech] are like persons brought in from outside for the purpose of exposition. A father does not act as go-between for his own son because the praises of the father would not be as effective as the praises of an outsider. It is the fault of other men, not mine [that I must resort to such a device, for if I were to speak in my own words], then men would respond only to what agrees with their own views and reject what does not, would pronounce "right" what agrees with their own views and "wrong" what does not. [303]

By "repeated words," the *Chuang Tzu* means a style of speech that appeals to the undisputed, universal authority of wise elders and, in so doing, establishes its own authority:

> These repeated words which make up seven tenths of it [i.e. the speech] are intended to put an end to argument. They can do this because they are the words of the elders. [303]

That these "repeated words" are a rhetorical device is demonstrated by the fact that the *Chuang Tzu* does not believe that the wise elders could faithfully transmit what they wanted to say, for, as explained in Chapter Three (Section k.), words alone cannot render justice to the meaning they purport to convey:

> "This book Your Grace is reading — may I venture to ask whose words are in it?"
> "The words of the sages," said the duke.
> "Are the sages still alive?"

"Dead long ago," said the duke.

"In that case, what you are reading there is nothing but the chaff and dregs of the men of old! . . . When the men of old died, they took with them the things [i.e. the meaning] that couldn't be handed down. So what you are reading there must be nothing but the chaff and dregs of the men of old." [152–53]

According to the *Chuang Tzu*, on the plane of speech, pain-avoidance is best achieved by means of "goblet words," which it defines as speech that harmonizes everything in Heavenly Equality:

> With these goblet words that come forth day after day, I harmonize all things in the Heavenly Equality, leave them to their endless changes, and so live out my years. [304]

But Heavenly Equality is the supreme wisdom of the universe, as well as Oneness and Sameness (Sixth and Seventh Cycles of the Way). Consequently, "goblet words" is a speech that equalizes in a positive way all opposite points of view and, as such, is both a detached and positive speech:

> Things all must have that which is so; things all must have that which is acceptable. There is nothing that is not so, nothing that is not acceptable. If there were no goblet words coming forth day after day to harmonize all by the Heavenly Equality, then how could I survive for long? [304]

In turn, a positive equalization of all opposite points of view is an obliteration of their definitions:

> Therefore the sage . . . illuminates all in the light of Heaven. He too recognizes a "this", but a "this" which is also "that", a "that" which is also "this". His "that" has both a right and a wrong in it; his "this" too has both a right and a wrong in it. So, in fact, does he still have a "this" and "that"? Or does he in fact no longer have a "this" and "that"? [40]

Again, definitions are expressed in words. It stands to reason, therefore, that the obliteration of definitions by means of a positive equalization of all opposite points of view is also the obliteration of words-as-definitions. For this reason, the *Chuang Tzu* calls "goblet words," that is to say, the speech that effects such an equalization, "words that are no-words." [304] Moreover, since "goblet words" is a speech without words-as-definitions, they express non-definitions, that is, Generality (see Chapter Three, Section i.). As such, "goblet words" is a speech that is so vague, so fluid and so imprecise in its formulation as to be a speech that says nothing *in particular*. Conversely, not to speak "goblet words" is to say plenty about *the whole of Generality*! This last point is not necessarily facetious, for the *Chuang Tzu* stresses the fact that truth is in the Generality, and that no words can express it, for words are partialization of Generality, as a whole, and, as such, a destruction of the Truth (see Chapter Three, Section k.):

> Therefore I say, we must have no-words! With words that are no-words, you may speak all your life long and you will never have said anything. Or you may go through your whole life *without* speaking them, in which case you will never have stopped speaking. [304]

This detailed investigation of the meaning of "goblet words" is necessary, for it helps to explain their quaint name. Indeed, a goblet is a vessel and, as such, can either be empty or full. In the light of what has just been said above, when "goblet words" are uttered, they say nothing and, consequently, are "empty" words. On the other hand, when "goblet words" are not spoken they preserve the integrity of the Generality that expresses the Truth and, as such, are "full" words. Hence their name.

Finally, the above investigation of the meaning of "goblet words" explains why they represent a pain-avoiding speech. Indeed, since he is mentally focussed on Generality, which in turn is an ample conviviality of many different and opposed points of view, the speaker of "goblet words" is a non-partisan speaker, who, in fact, welcomes any new opinion and judgment on the part of his interlocutors, for he is ever eager to add them to his Generality. And to be non-partisan and to welcome the opinions and judgments of others is a sure way of avoiding their resentment.

162

AFTERWORD: ALMOST A MANIFESTO

This book on the *Chuang Tzu* is my second venture into self-styled structural analysis. By self-styled structural analysis, I mean a structural analysis that is strictly authorized by the text itself, and not "read into" with the help of preconceived notions. My first venture was the structural analysis of the ideology of the Russian, religious Utopian thinker, N.F. Fedorov (1828–1903). The only thing that my two books have in common is that they deal with two allegedly impossible topics. Indeed, it has been a firm tenet of faith among academic pundits that neither the ideology of Fedorov nor that of the *Chuang Tzu* could be grasped as well-defined philosophical systems. In both cases, my self-styled structural analysis proved that it was not so, thus establishing its authority as a valuable tool of intellectual investigation. For that reason, I feel obliged to say a few words about what I think are the potentials of my method.

This book and my book on Fedorov offer but a limited experience in the field of self-styled structural analysis. Yet, they have demonstrated, and not merely pre-supposed, that two entirely different ideologies have two entirely different structures. Indeed, the structure of Fedorov's ideology is a three-stranded helix that coils itself around four evolutionary columns, whereas as illustrated above, the structure of the ideology of the *Chuang Tzu* is the cycle of man's consciousness, circumscribed by the greater cycle of the Way of Heaven and Earth, in which man's consciousness is the microcosm of the Way of Heaven and Earth, which, in turn, is the macrocosm of man's consciousness. It was the interpenetrability of these two cycles that accounts for the interchangeability between the cosmic force of yang and Reality-consciousness and the cosmic force of yin and Self-consciousness. This seemingly obvious discovery of the fact that two different ideologies have two different structures is nonetheless fraught with incalculable theoretical significance.

163

Indeed, if these two different ideologies have two different structures, then does it mean generally that there are as many potential different structures as there are different ideologies? In such a case, would it be possible to find among all these different structures, representing contentually different ideologies, geometrical affinities? If so, what would be the significance of these geometrical affinities between structures that represent contentually different ideologies? Conversely, supposing that one were to discover that contentually kindred ideologies have structures that have no geometrical affinities with one another, what significance such a lack of geometrical affinity would have on the respective meaning of these kindred ideologies? Or their semantics?

Or, is there a limited number of structures for all ideologies? In this case, would this limited number of structures describe the "intellectual vocabulary" of the brain? Or, just the limitation of the brain's intellectual vocabulary? If so, would such an investigation point out to some neglected possibilities, and raise the question of the reasons for such an intellectual blindness?

Again, what would the study of the ideological structures of the ideologies of people living in the same historical period, the same geographical area, the same cultural ambient and, presumably sharing the same qualities of education and consciousness, yield? Would there be more affinity between such structures, or not? And, if such an "horizontal" study were not conclusive, would it not be better to classify all these contemporary ideologies according to groups sharing structural affinities, and by comparing these ideologies within each group discover the norms of relationship that may possibly exist between the structure and the content of thought? And, by taking up the same problem "vertically," that is to say historically, would it be possible to discover an evolutionary pattern to the structures of kindred ideologies?

Finally, by discovering the national predilections for certain ideological structures, would it be possible to understand more thoroughly the essence of foreign modes of expression such as culture, worldview, politics, society, and so on?

Ostensibly, all these questions represent a vast program for mapping the yet-unchartered areas of the human brain in its individual, historical and cultural complexity. Since all these questions sprang up naturally out of my two works in the field of self-styled structural analysis, I believe that self-styled structural analysis can be a valuable means to that end.

BOOKS CITED IN THE TEXT

Creel, H.G. *What is Taoism? and Other Studies in Chinese Cultural History* (The University of Chicago Press, Chicago and London, 1970).

Lloyd, G.E.R. *Polarity and Analogy* (Cambridge University Press, 1966).

Needham, J. *Science and Civilization in China* (Cambridge University Press, 1956) Vol II.

Rank, O. *Grundzüge einer genetischen Psychologie auf Grund der Psychoanalyse der Ich. Struktur, Vol I: Genetische Psychologie; Vol II: Gestaltung und Ausdruck der Persönlichkeit* (Deuticke Verlag, Vienna, 1927 and 1928).

———. *Will Therapy and Truth and Reality* (Alfred Knopf: New York, 1964).

Seung, T.K. *Structuralism and Hermeneutics* (Columbia University Press, New York, 1982).

Waley, A. *Three Ways of Thought in Ancient China* (G. Allen and Unwin Ltd., London, 1946).

INDEX

Richard, H. Schlagel

FROM MYTH TO THE MODERN MIND

A Study of the Origins and the Growth of Scientific Thought
Volume I: Animism to Archimedes

American University Studies: Series V (Philosophy). Vol. 12
ISBN 0-8204-0219-2   281 pp.   hardback US $ 30.00*

*Recommended price - alterations reserved

Written before the collapse of the research program of the logical posi-
tivists and the resurgent interest in the development of scientific thought
as exemplivied in analyses of actual historical transitions, this book is unique
in undertaking to elucidate the   *cognitive developments and their causes*
underlying the history of science. Beginning with a description of forms of
primitive mentality, as exemplified historically in the earlier animistic, mythopoetic, and theogonic traditions, the present volume identifies the transformations in the *thought processes* inherent in the emergence and the growth
of scientific rationalism from the Presocraties thought Plato and Aristotle to
Archimedes, the culminating scientific figure in the ancient world.

Contents: The purpose of the present volume is to contrast scientific rationalism with the earlier animistic, mythopoetic, and theogonic traditions, trac-
ing the origins and the growth of scientific thought in the works of the
Presocraties, Plato and Aristotle, to Archimedes.

PETER LANG PUBLISHING, INC.
62 West 45th Street
USA - New York, NY 10036

Charles M. Natoli

NIETZSCHE AND PASCAL ON CHRISTIANITY

American University Studies: Series V, (Philosophy). Vol. 3
ISBN 0-8204-0071-8   197 pages   hardback US $ 24.25*

*Recommended price – alterations reserved

Although Pascal was one of the small group of thinkers who influenced Nietzsche profoundly, and although Nietzsche claimed to have Pascal's blood running in his veins, Pascal did not succeed in getting him to share his intense preoccupation with the question of the truth of Christian belief. Not its truth but the value of its effects on mankind became the focus of Nietzsche's vitriolic anti-Christian polemics. This study, one of the very few on the Nietzsche/Pascal relationship, explores and appreciates the religious thought of each. It also assesses the nature and ground of their relationship and investigates the reasonableness of the Faith that divided them.

Contents: A study of the relationship of Pascal to Nietzsche and of their disparate approaches to the problems each saw posed by Christianity. In particular, should considerations of truth or of value be paramount in appraising religious belief?

PETER LANG PUBLISHING, INC.
62 West 45th Street
USA – New York, NY 10036